Literature-Based
Geography Activities
AN INTEGRATED APPROACH
TARA McCARTHY

SCHOLASTIC
PROFESSIONAL BOOKS

New York · Toronto · London · Auckland · Sydney

Thanks to

Linda Common, School Librarian in Chester, New York, who provided invaluable help in selecting books that exemplify the literature-geography connection

and

Jane Neher Keefe, pre-school and kindergarten director, The Country Mouse School, Woodstock, New York, for her advice and feedback on books and activities for beginning readers

Designed by Nancy Metcalf
Production by Intergraphics
Cover design by Vincent Ceci
Cover illustration by Beth Glick
Illustrations by Joe Chicko, Terri Chicko

ISBN 0-590-49184-9

Contents

Introduction

Using Literature to Build Geography Skills and Concepts

Good books have geography built into them. As children and adults read literature, they focus on a classic quartet of ingredients: character, theme, plot, and *setting. Setting* is geography. Where does the story take place? How do the landforms and water and climate of that place influence the characters' actions? How do characters in books change the places they live, use its resources, and form links with people in other places? The characters in children's literature are greatly shaped by the nature of the place in which they live (physical geography) and the changes they and other people make in these places (human geography).

You've probably been using literature to teach geography all along. For example, when reading Laura Ingalls Wilder's *Little House* books with your students, discussions gravitate toward the geographical settings of prairie and forest. Cutting and hewing trees, building a house, planting the land, coping with unfamiliar weather and the vast distances that sometimes separate families for months at a time—all these geographical phenomena lead to the shaping of character, the themes of endurance and change, and lively plots which involve making-do and adapting to new geographical settings.

Literature-Based Geography Activities **is designed to help your students build specific geography skills and concepts as they read fine literature.** As students learn the skills of mapping and charting, comparing and contrasting, graphing and diagramming, they are better able to clarify and communicate their geographic understandings. These skills will serve your students well as they work through your social studies curriculum. Just as important, through developing these skills students will appreciate more thoroughly the importance of *setting* to the characters in the books they read and thus be able to relate these books thoughtfully to the way their own day-to-day experiences are affected by the settings in which they themselves live now, and which they will help to shape in the future.

Using *Literature-Based Geography Activities*

The Literature: Twenty-four books have been selected. Titles 1–6 are of special appeal to students in Kindergarten and first grade (Picture Book level). Titles 7–16 are for students who have a reading/comprehension level of approximately Grade 1–Grade 2 (Story Book level). Titles 17–24 are for students reading and comprehending at grade levels 3–4 (Chapter Book level).

The Format: For each book, two pages are directed to you and two are reproducibles you can invite students to use. The pages for you, the teacher, follow this sequence:
• A **Story Summary.**
• **Preparation** suggestions (for example, getting necessary maps).
• **As You Read** suggestions for (1.) directing students' attention to the geography or other concept or skill designated for study in the book; (2.) helping students to respond personally to the story.
• A suggestion for **Extending Geography Skills** through hands-on skills activities that build on the concepts students have developed by reading the book.
• Several suggestions for **Making Connections** through geography to creative and "practice" writing, math, science, thinking skills, and other curriculum areas.
   The student activity pages are designed for independent use. The first centers on the geography skill or concept; the second on a related understanding about literature, such as character development or sequence.

Teaching and Learning Strategies: There are abundant suggestions here for **cooperative learning activities, partner-team activities and investigations,** ways to involve the **whole class,** and for **individual activities** that many students will enjoy carrying out on their own and then sharing with the class. There is a multitude of **bulletin board** ideas that invite students to interact with and contribute to visual interpretations of what they are learning.

A Range of Options for Teachers and Students: Dip and choose! Any of the concepts and skills and the related activities presented in *Literature-Based Geography Activities* can be taken up whenever you feel they would be most useful and timely in your social studies curriculum. While the literature is ordered according to reading/comprehension level, the concepts and skills can be taught and introduced or reviewed with integrity at any of the grade levels covered. Refer to the **Additional Resources** list on pages 108–112 for suggestions about literature you might use to introduce or review a skill or concept on a lower or higher level.

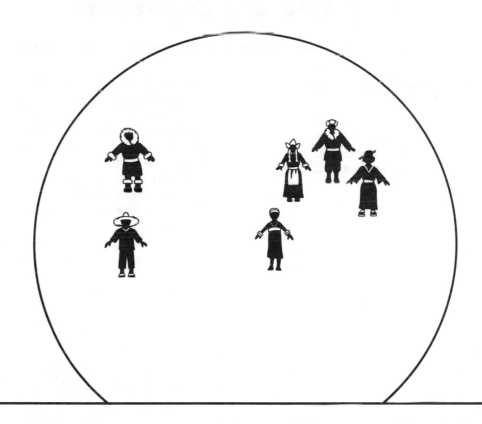

 **Picture Book Level**

Katy and the Big Snow

Virginia Lee Burton (Houghton Mifflin 1971)

Summary:

After a heavy snow, Katy—a crawler tractor—plows out the streets of the city of Geoppolis so that basic services can get back into operation.

Preparation:

Make several copies of the map on pages 6–7. As you show the book cover and read the title, point out the initials (K.T.) on the bulldozer/snowplow, and explain that they stand for *crawler tractor* (with the initial *k* standing for the /k/ sound in *crawler.*) Have pupils say the /k/ and /t/ together to figure out how Katy got her name.

As You Read:

Encourage students to get information from small pictures by discussing and reading the picture-frames on pages 1–5. For example, ask students to (1.) figure out how the pictures of 55 horses on page 1 help them to understand how strong Katy is; (2.) decide which signs and machines on pages 4–5 they have seen in their own community and how these signs and machines help traffic flow.

To direct reading, distribute the copies of the picture map before you discuss pages 6–7 and use the map for informal games as the reading progresses. Here are some sample map-reading games:

1. *Pages 6–7:* Play a brief warm-up game in which (1.) students say "Katy goes to (numeral on map)," and you point out the corresponding picture and read its label. (2.) You read the marginal numeral and label and ask students to find that numeral on the map. For example: "Katy goes to 17, the freight yard. Find 17, the freight yard, on the map."

2. *Pages 18–32:* Ask students to refer to their copies of the picture map to find the places named: Police Department (3); Post Office (10); Railway Station (19); Telephone Company (21); Electric Company (20); Water Department (24); Hospital (26); Fire Department (27). You might also ask students to decide which numeral (31, after 30, the Piggery) should indicate the airport, which is shown at the top of the map but has no numeral there. Have students write *31* in the appropriate place on their copies of the picture map.

3. *Pages 34–35:* Encourage students to collate their maps with the pictures so that they can name some of the places shown in the illustration.

To guide reading, use "what-how" questions throughout to get at cause-and-effect. Make a circle diagram of the major points, with students filling in the circles as they listen to the story.

What Happens?	**How Does It Change Things?**
A heavy snow falls.	All the roads are blocked.
Katy plows the roads.	Traffic can move.
The doctor can get to a sick person.	The sick person gets well.

Extending Geography Skills: Cardinal Directions

1. **Which Way is North?** *(learning direction words)* On the chalkboard, draw a compass rose like the one below. Using a compass, adapt your drawing so that it is tilted to true north in relation to your classroom.

Use a globe as you point out the North and South poles. Let students examine a compass as you explain that the needle always points north (toward the North Pole). Refer to the compass rose as you point out how *west* is to your left, *east* is to your right, and *south* directly behind you when you face *north*.

To help pupils orient themselves, ask them to stand with outstretched arms, face north, south, east, or west as you direct, and tell what classroom fixtures or items lie in the other directions, using the direction words or the phrases *to my left, to my right,* and *behind me*.

Suggest that partners play a game in which "It" is Katy and the other player uses direction words to tell Katy how many steps in different directions to move to reach various locations in the classroom or on the playground.

2. **Katy's Travels** *(using a compass rose)* Make copies of the compass rose (p. 8) and give one to each student. Have students paste the copy on oaktag, cut it out, and color the initial letters (N, S, E, W). Ask students to place their compass roses on their copies of the picture map, with *north* in the same position as in the book. Reread pages 23–30 and invite pupils to name some of the places in East, North, West, and South Geoppolis. Discuss how the direction words help Katy know exactly where to go to plow the roads.

Small groups of students can use their map-copies and compass roses to pose and answer questions about the location of different places in Geoppolis.

Making Connections

Social Studies:

A New-Friend Map Students can contribute to a bulletin-board map of the school neighborhood that would be useful to a new classmate. Take students on a tour of the neighborhood, supplying student-partners with a map outline with your school at the center and a compass rose at the corner. Ask partners to note on their maps important sites to the north, south, east, and west of the school. Back in the classroom, ask students to use their notes to draw pictures and write labels to place correctly on a *KATY WELCOMES YOU* bulletin board.

Literature

1. **Cause and Effect** Reread page 15 of the story and discuss why things came to a standstill in Geoppolis. Use a chalkboard *If . . . Then* chart to help students think about what might have happened if Katy had not been there to save the day.

IF	THEN
The mail can't go through	people don't get their letters.
Fire engines can't move	buildings burn down
Electric wires fall down	houses have no lights

Invite students to copy and illustrate a sentence from the If-Then Chart. Put the completed sentences and drawings in a folder on a reading table for students to read and discuss independently.

2. **Picture-map Settings** Pupils can work together in small groups to make picture-maps showing important places in other stories. You might launch the activity by showing the picture map in A. A. Milne's *Winnie the Pooh* and comparing it with the map in *Katy and the Big Snow*. Group-member assignments can include: planning together; drawing the pictures; writing the labels; showing the picture map to classmates and telling about a story incident that happened in each place.

Creative Writing:

Thank You, Katy! Ask students to imagine they live in Geoppolis. Ask them to write notes to Katy to thank her for some special way she helped them during the snowstorm.

Katy's Friend Helps Out

1. Make a picture map. In each frame, draw something outside your school building.

2. Cut out the snowplow and move it from place to place on your map. Tell how it can help in each place.

Help, Katy!

Cut out each card and paste it on cardboard. On the other side draw a picture of what Katy does to help. Make up some **Help, Katy!** card games to play with your friends.

Ming Lo Moves the Mountain

Arnold Lobel (Scholastic 1982)

Summary:

Ming Lo and his wife are unhappy living under a mountain and follow a wise man's suggestions about ways to move it. After attempts to push, scare, and coax the mountain fail to work, the wise man suggests that the couple take the house apart and carry the materials as they do a ritual dance with their eyes closed. The dance takes them far away from the mountain, but Ming Lo and his wife—happy at last!—believe it is the mountain that has finally moved!

Preparation:

After showing the book cover and reading the title, discuss with pupils why someone might want to move a mountain and why this would be impossible for a person to do. Encourage pupils to predict various fanciful ways in which Ming Lo might try to move a mountain.

As You Read

Use a chalkboard chart like the one below as you direct the pupils' reading. Call on pupils for phrases or sentences to fill in the chart as the story progresses.

Wise Man's Suggestion	Did it work?	Why or why not?
Push with a tree.	No.	A person pushing a tree isn't strong enough to move a mountain.
Make lots of noise.	No.	A mountain isn't a person, so you can't scare it.
Take gifts to the mountain.	No.	The wind blew the cakes and bread away.
Take your house apart and do a special dance.	Yes.	The dance moved Ming Lo and his wife away from the mountain.

Guide reading by asking questions like these:

1. What problems do Ming Lo and his wife have with their house under the mountain? How could they solve these problems without trying to move the mountain? (For example: build a stronger roof; get a wood stove to heat the house; find a field away from the mountain's shadow in which to grow a garden.)

2. Is the wise man really wise? Does he really think that his first three suggestions will work, or is he just trying to show Ming Lo the impossibility of moving a mountain?

3. What do you think about the wise man's final suggestion? Is he playing a trick on Ming Lo? Is he trying to help him?

4. If you were a friend of Ming Lo, what would you tell him when he says "The mountain has moved far away."?

Extending Geography Skills: Topographical Maps

1. **Ming Lo's Land** (*making relief maps*)   Pupils can work in groups of four or five to make a relief map to show the key places in the story setting. Provide each group with a sheet of heavy corrugated cardboard, the kind appliances are packed in, for a base; clay or plasticine for molding landforms; tempera paint and brushes; markers, paper strips and glue for making labels. Group-member assignments might include: (1.) sketching out on the plywood the positions of the mountain, the first location of Ming Lo's house, the Wise Man's house, and the second location of Ming Lo's house; (2.) using the book illustration for ideas, sketching in other geographic features (trees, the village, smaller hills); (3.) molding these structures from clay; (4.) deciding on and using specific colors to indicate mountains, hills, valleys, rivers and lakes; (5.) painting in black the footsteps of Ming Lo and his wife as they moved their house; (6.) writing labels for the table-top map.

    Groups can use doll-house miniatures or pipe-cleaner figures to act out the story of Ming Lo in their relief-map settings.

2. **Moving Ming Lo** (*using a topographical map*)
Display a topographical map of your state or of the United States. Help students to find the area where they live and to figure out how colors and shading are used to show water, high land areas, and low land areas. Discuss how the map is like their table-top relief maps (in its use of color to show water and land forms) and how it is different (the topographical map is flat).

Then provide students with gummed circles to represent Ming Lo and have them take turns moving the circles on the map to show regions where Ming Lo, who dislikes mountains, would like to live and areas where he would not like to live.

3. **Up and Down the Neighborhood** Based on their day-to-day experiences or on a class walking tour, students can make a neighborhood topographical picture map to show hills, flat areas, woods or parks, and streams, ponds, or rivers. Suggest that students label their maps to make them useful to a new student in their school. Display the maps on a bulletin board or put them in a folder for students to study and enjoy independently.

Making Connections

Social Studies:
Land and Water Around the World Have students help you make a bulletin-board display showing the land and water forms of either the places from which the students themselves recently moved or the places from which their families came. Students can base their pictures on memories, photographs, or interviews they conduct with family members. Write labels to identify the students and—as closely as possible—the names of the places they show in their pictures. Invite students to take turns telling about these places on the basis of their own memories or the recollections of their families. If possible, use a topographical map of the country or of continents to pinpoint the locations as students discuss the places. Encourage the classroom audience to tell why they would like to visit the places their classmates describe. Discuss how the land forms and bodies of water contrast and compare with the ones in your community.

Literature:
Solving Problems Review what Ming Lo's problem was and how the problem was solved. Discuss the problems of characters in other stories the students have recently read. List the characters and their problems on a *Solving Problems* chart.

Complete the Solutions column of the chart by asking students to take turns playing the part of the Wise Man in *Ming Lo Moves the Mountain* and telling the character how to solve his or her problem.

Character	Problem	Solution
Winnie-the-Pooh	gets stuck in Rabbit's door	Lose some weight by not eating.
Little Red Hen	can't get friends to help make bread	Do all the work yourself.
Mother Duck and ducklings	need to get across busy street to pond	Have a policeman stop the traffic.

To emphasize the role that the problem plays in a good story, ask students if they can think of a story that does **not** have a problem in it.

Creative Writing:
More Problems for Ming Lo Students can work in small groups to write and illustrate their own stories about Ming Lo. Ask groups to imagine that Ming Lo lives in one of the locations listed below. Their stories can tell (1.) why he and his wife do not like the place, and (2.) how they solve their problem.

Places: the seashore; a forest; a desert; on a mountain top. Invite groups to read and show their finished stories to the class or to act them out. Put the stories in a folder on a reading table for students to look at and discuss independently.

Movement and Dance:
Steps and Splashes Call on a volunteer to choose from a chalkboard list of land forms and bodies of water, and—without revealing the choice—pantomine the way Ming Lo would move through or across this area. The volunteer can select three or four classmates to follow-the-leader, then ask them or other classmates to tell where their pantomime trip has taken them. What movement-clues did the audience or followers use to make their guess?

Math:
Measuring Heights and Depths Ask student-partners to use the relief key on a topographical map to figure out how shades of colors are used to show more precisely the different altitudes of land and depth of water. Have partners explain to classmates what colors might be used to show Ming Lo's mountain and the place where his house is.

13

Ming Lo's Places

1. In the blanks, write names for the places.
2. In the boxes, write some words that describe the place.
3. Color the pictures.
4. Cut along the dotted lines. Fold on the solid lines.
5. On the blank side, draw or write more about Ming Lo.

Mount _____

Fold A

Fold B

_____ Forest

Lake _____

Name _____

Help Ming Lo and his wife put their house back together again.

1. Cut out the house parts. Paste them on a sheet of paper to make a house. Add your own colors, lines, and ideas.

2. Cut around your house. Leave tabs to fold so that the house will stand up.

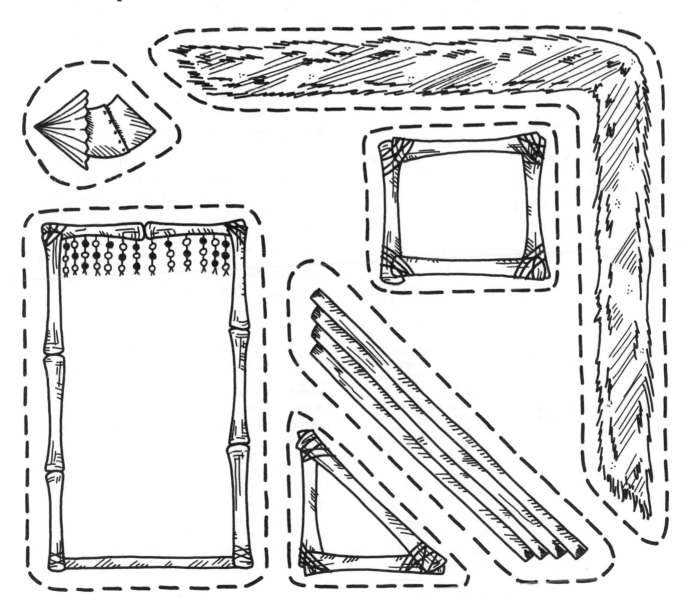

The Little House

Virginia Lee Burton (Houghton Mifflin 1969)

Summary:

Through many years, the Little House watches as the farmland and countryside around her give way to the growing city. She is eventually abandoned by her family and stands run-down and unhappy in the midst of tall buildings and busy traffic. Finally a great-great granddaughter of the original builder finds the Little House, moves her way out into the country, and restores her. Once again the Little House is lived in, cared for, and happy.

Preparation:

As you show the book cover and read the title, also read and point out the word *Her-story* and discuss how this is based on the word *history*. Explain that *history* means the story of things that happen over time. Ask students to predict what might happen to the Little House as time goes by.

As You Read

Direct students' attention to the different kinds of changes that happen over time, as shown in the pictures. As the story progresses, students can use picture clues to help them fill in a chart like the one below:

Time	Change	How We Measure It
day and night	light and dark	clocks
seasons and months	weather; trees and other plants	calendars, thermometers
years	cities grow; people grow up; ways of life change; new inventions	histories, pictures, photographs

Guide reading by asking questions like these:

1. What changes does the Little House notice as day turns to night and as the seasons go by? Why is she used to these changes? You may wish to introduce the term *cycles* and explain how they imply regularity and the expected.

2. How do horseless carriages, trucks, and steam shovels change the surroundings of the Little House? How do you think she feels about these changes? How fast do you think these changes happen: overnight? in one year? over many years?

As a reading-response strategy, invite students to make up dialogue for the Little House as the city is growing around her. Suggest that her words tell about the changes she sees and how she feels about these changes.

Extending Geography Skills: Time Lines

Do You Have the Time? Pupils can work in groups of four or five to make an illustrated timeline showing changes in the Little House's environment. As a way of introducing the activity, draw a timeline on the chalkboard and call on students to suggest what pictures could be drawn to illustrate each segment on it.

Time: the Seasons

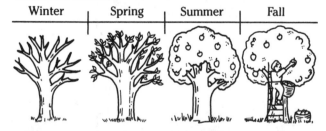

| Winter | Spring | Summer | Fall |

Invite the class to brainstorm a list of other changes shown in the story and the illustrations. Examples are: morning, afternoon, evening, night; seasonal changes in people's work and play; changes in the Little House's appearance; changes in the buildings surrounding the Little House; changes in tools, machines, and transportation; changes in the Little House's feelings.

Have each group choose a time-and-change idea to illustrate on its time line. Assignments can include: drawing the time line and allotting space for each drawing; making the pictures; writing labels; proofreading and correcting; showing the finished time line to the class.

16

Making Connections

Social Studies:

Grow a City   As a hands-on exercise in changing the environment, place a picture of the Little House in the center of the board. Invite students to take turns each day adding a cut-paper building to the display. Have students label their buildings to show what they are used for (apartments, offices, factories, museums, etc.). As buildings are added, discuss what other changes will happen around the Little House as a result (more people, more traffic, more services, etc.).

Literature and Writing:

Little House Comics   Invite students to make picture strips with dialogue balloons to retell the Little House's story in sequence. After students show and read their completed story-strips, put the strips in a *Little House Comics* folder for students to read and discuss independently.

Oral Language:

Walks and Talks   Invite a long-time resident to join your class in a field trip to explore changes that have happened in your community over the years. Ask this community-resource person to point out places that have changed greatly, for example, the shopping mall that used to be a field of daisies, or the tidy row of apartments in what used to be a vacant lot. Back in the classroom, ask volunteers to draw and make captions for before-and-after pictures to put in a folder on a reading table.

Science:

Recording Changes   Students can keep daily world-and-picture-charts to note changes in everyday phenomena like the following: weather; foliage; development of classroom flora and fauna, such as bean seeds, guppies, and hamsters; different numbers and kinds of birds that come to a feeder outside the window, depending upon the kind of seed distributed. Post the charts and use them for discussing sequence and time.

Math:

Choosing Measuring Tools   Display a wide variety of tools that can be used to measure and keep track of time and change. Examples are: stopwatches, calendars, clocks, hour (or minute)-sand-glasses, sundials, metronomes, cooking-timer-buzzers, height charts, weight scales, copies of old and new maps or old and new photographs of the same place. Have students work with a partner to figure how each tool measures time. Ask students to report their findings to the class by telling how the Little House's family might use the tool.

17

Name _____

Imagine you are a Little House. In each window, draw something different you see each day.

Cut out the flaps. Paste the flaps along the top of each window to make a window shade. Put the flaps down. See if your classmates can guess the pictures underneath.

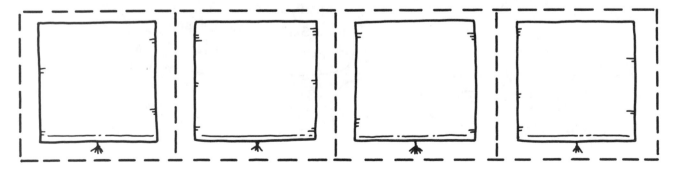

Name _____

Shuffle Stories

1. Color the pictures and cut them out.
2. Put the pictures face down. Choose two or three.
3. Make up a story to go with the pictures you chose.

Nine-In-One Grr! Grrr!

Blia Xiong and Cathy Spagnoli
Illustrated by Nancy Hom
(Children's Book Press 1989)

Summary:

In this folktale from the Hmong people of Laos, a tiger travels to the kingdom of the Sky God, Shao, to find out how many cubs she will have. Shao says the tiger will have nine cubs each year, but only if she remembers the words "nine-in-one." A Eu bird, alarmed at how a fast-growing tiger population might eat up all the other animals, distracts the tiger as she sings her formula, so that she begins to sing "one-in-nine." (one cub in nine years). This, says the tale, is why there are so few tigers in the world.

Preparation:

Point out Laos on a map or globe as you explain where the story comes from. Ask students to predict whether all the wild animals they will see in the pictures will be ones they can see around their community. Encourage children to give reasons for their predictions.

As You Read

Direct reading by asking students to look and listen for animals and plants the pictures and story tell about and to decide whether or not they are native to their own area. These can be listed on a chart like the one below. Use the chart as a basis for discussing how wildlife varies from region to region. Invite students to share what they know about animals in other parts of the world, such as penguins in Antarctica and koala bears in Australia.

Animal or Plant	In Laos	Where We Live
tiger	yes	no
tortoise	yes	yes
monkey	yes	no
banana trees	yes	no
rabbit	yes	yes

Guide reading by asking questions like these:
1. What parts of the story are make-believe (talking tigers; lands in the sky, etc.) What parts are real? (animals and plants of Laos; tigers having cubs, etc.)
2. Why is the Eu Bird upset at the idea of a tiger having nine cubs each year?
3. What happens because of Tiger forgetting the words Shao taught her?

As reading-response strategies (1.) Invite students to discuss whether they think the Eu Bird was right or wrong in tricking Tiger. Encourage students to give reasons for their opinions. (2.) Ask students to recall how the story explains why there are so few tigers in the world. Have students decide whether this reason is factual or make-believe.

Extending Geography Skills: Wildlife Map

Find Out and Draw It. Through field trips to the playground and nearby parks and wildlife sanctuaries, through library research, and by listening to community resource people involved in wildlife management and ecology, children can find out about wildlife native to the area in which they live. Invite students to make pictures of and labels for insects, birds, reptiles, amphibians, and mammals native to your state. Attach these drawings and labels to a bulletin-board state outline map. Ask students to tell about the animals they have actually seen and to discuss why the others are a rarer sight. For example, the animals may live in special environments, such as marshes; or they may be rare or endangered species.

Making Connections

Literature:
Story Maps Review the story and ask partners to make an illustrated story map to show (1.) Tiger's home, (2.) the road that goes from her home to Shao's land, (3.) Shao's land in the sky. Invite partners to tell what happens in each place as

they show their maps to classmates. Put the story maps in a folder on a reading table for students to share and discuss.

Creative Writing:
Here's How it Happened! Students can work in groups of four or five to write and illustrate origin stories about how wild animals in their area came to have a particular characteristic. Examples are: "Why Squirrels Have Bushy Tails," "Why Racoons Have Black Masks," "Why Deer Are Shy." After planning the story together, group members can assign roles: two or three members to draw incidents in the story; two or three members to write the words; one member to make a cover for the story. After groups have read and shown their stories to the class, put the stories on a reading table for students to enjoy independently.

Math:
Finger Tigers Students can learn to multiply 1 × 9 through 9 × 9 by using the "finger strategy" described below. Then they can use the strategy to figure out how many cubs the tiger would have in one year, two years, and so forth to nine years if she actually had nine cubs each year. (The strategy works only with the number nine, due to special characteristics of that number.)

1. Put hands palms down. Starting with the little finger of the left hand, use a charcoal pencil to number your fingers from 1 to 10.

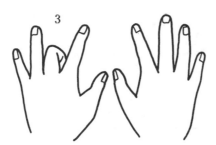

2. To multiply nine by a number from 1 to 9, first bend the finger with that number.

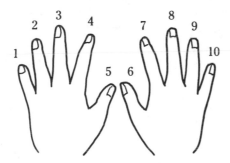

What is 9 × 3?
Bend the "3" finger

3. Now count the fingers to the left of the bent finger. Write the number of fingers. Now count the fingers to the right of the bent finger. Write that number of fingers after the first one. The result is the answer to the "9-times" problem.

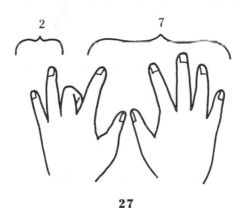

27

Fingers to the left: 2
Fingers to the right: 7
9 × 3 = 27

Language:
What's It Like? To help students hone their skill of observing the natural world, reread page 4 of the book and ask students to find in the picture "plants curved like rooster tails" and "rocks shaped like sleeping giants." Discuss other comparisons the picture suggests, for example, "clouds curled like snails" and "a butterfly like a flying flower." Take students on a tour of a park and ask them to use comparisons as they point out and tell about animals, plants, and rocks. Jot down or tape record their comparisons and, back in the classroom, transcribe them to the chalkboard or to poster paper. Invite students to copy and illustrate the comparisons they like best. Display the work around the room, then suggest that students take their comparisons home to share with their families.

Animals of Laos

1. Color the animals and cut them out.
2. Paste the animals on a sheet of colored paper. Draw a beautiful border around your picture.
3. Cut out the labels. Ask a classmate to match each label to an animal in your picture.

monkey	bird	barking deer
tiger	green-striped snake	rooster

A Brand New Animal!

1. Cut out the pieces. Paste some on a sheet of paper to make a make-believe animal.
2. Color your picture.
3. Make up a name for your animal.
4. Tell a story about how the animal came to be.

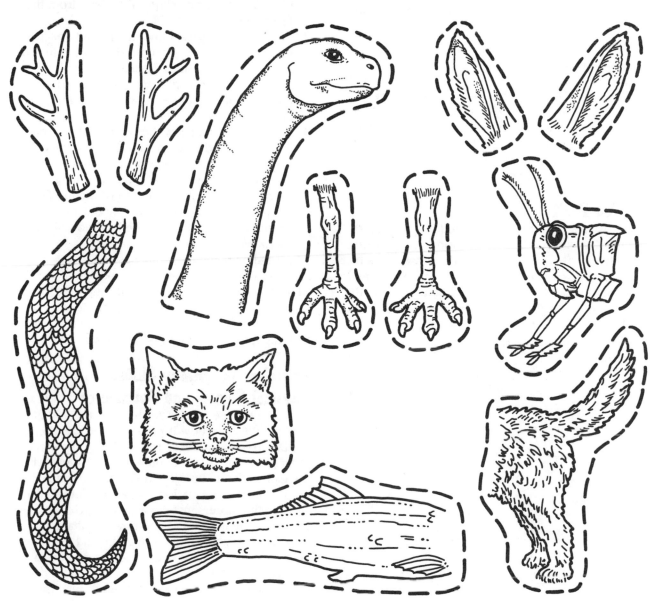

Where the Forest Meets the Sea

Jeannie Baker (Greenwillow Books, 1987)

Summary:

A boy goes by boat with his father to a rainforest on the northeast shore of Australia. There the boy explores the primeval woods and waterways, imagines what it must have been like to live there eons ago, and thinks about what might happen to the forest in the future.

Preparation:

As you show the book cover, ask students to point out the sea, the beach, the forest, and the tiny boat. Explain that the boy in the boat will explore a forest that is millions of years old. Ask students to predict what he will see and how he will feel. Write predictions on poster paper to refer to and discuss when you have finished reading.

As You Read

Direct reading by encouraging students to explore the vivid illustrations to brainstorm a list of words and phrases that describe what the boy sees as he looks at the sea, reef, beach, sky, creek, and forest. Students' responses can be listed on a web like the one below. Display the web as an idea resource for students to use as they retell the story.

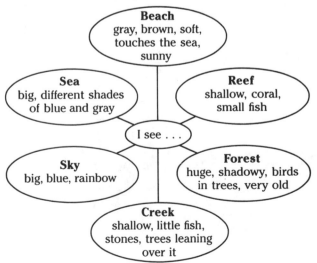

Beach
gray, brown, soft, touches the sea, sunny

Sea
big, different shades of blue and gray

Reef
shallow, coral, small fish

I see . . .

Sky
big, blue, rainbow

Forest
huge, shadowy, birds in trees, very old

Creek
shallow, little fish, stones, trees leaning over it

Guide reading with questions like these:
1. How does the boy get into the rainforest? (follows the creek from the sea). How are the banks of the creek different from the floor of the forest? (Vines and creepers grow along the creek bank; the forest floor is barer.) How do you explain this? (Discuss the effect of sunlight on plants: big trees shut out the sun from the forest floor.)
2. The boy really sees some things, and imagines others. How do the pictures show the things he imagines? (The things he sees in his mind's eye—like the crocodile, the dinosaur, and a future building project—are shown in a shadowy way.)
3. Point out the name of the boy's boat—"Time Machine"—and discuss why this name fits the story. (The boy's adventure leads him back in time.) Ask students why the boat name "Paradise Real Estate" in the last picture fits the prediction the boy makes about the future. (Houses may be built on the land now filled by the rainforest.)

As reading-response strategies (1.) invite students to suggest how they would feel and what they would wonder about if they were accompanying the boy on his explorations. (2.) Encourage students to discuss how the boy might feel if the rainforest is destroyed.

Extending Geography Skills: Physical Shapes and Boundaries

Show the outline map of Australia at the end of the book and discuss how it pinpoints the location of the Daintree Rainforest—the setting of the story. Then point out Australia on a globe. Discuss what the globe shows about Australia that the map does not (for example, location on Earth, relative size, surrounding waters, neighboring countries and continents, major cities) and how the shape of Australia is the same on both globe and map. On enlarged copies of the map, students can make picture or word lists of what they have learned about the Daintree Rainforest, then display their work around the room. To extend the activity, distribute outline maps of the United States and invite students to find this shape, their nation, on a globe. Suggest that student partners imagine they are traveling between Australia and the United States and use the globe to make up and answer oral questions about their voyage.

Making Connections

Literature/Art:

Collages and Captions   As students discuss the book illustrations, explain that they are photographs of collages: pictures made with different materials. Invite students to identify parts of the pictures that were made with modelling clay, different kinds of paper, fabric, sandpaper, paint, twigs, and leaves. On a field trip around a playground or park, cooperative learning groups of four or five students can collect natural materials to combine with classroom art materials to make a collage picture about their immediate environment. Group roles might include: two members to decide what event or area the picture will show; one or two members to arrange and glue the materials on a cardboard backing; one member to write a sentence caption for the collage. After groups have shown and shared their collages with the class, display the collages around the room. Discuss how and why the natural materials in the collages are different from the ones the Australian artist used in her book.

Vocabulary:

Name That Place!   Using an idea web like the one on page 24, students can brainstorm for precise words to name the geographic features of their area, such as *brook, river, riverbanks, woods,* *hill, valley,* and so forth. Encourage students to suggest words and phrases that describe each place. Students can practice and use the place-vocabulary by (1.) playing an oral Where-Am-I game in which they describe the place without naming it and ask classmates to guess the place; (2.) making paintings or drawings of the place and writing a caption to identify it; (3.) writing a descriptive poem about one of the places. Put drawings, paintings, and poems on a reading table in a folder titled *Our Places* for students to study and discuss with a partner independently.

Science:

Why Save the Rainforests?   In the center of the display, place a large drawing of trees, or an enlarged copy of one of the book illustrations. Place these labels around the centerpiece: *Important Plants; Conserving Water; Cleaning the Air; Rare Animals; A Home for People; Beauty.* Invite interested students to use reference books, the library, and data gleaned from TV documentaries—many of which are available on video tapes—to help you fill out each category with specifics, shown through students' words and pictures. Students can invite other classes or family members to view the finished display and discuss suggestions for saving the rainforests from further destruction. Students not directly involved in creating the display can make Save the Rainforest posters based on the information presented.

Rainforest Puzzler

1. Use four different colors to color the sea, the forest, the beach, and the creek.
2. Cut out the picture and paste it on cardboard.
3. Cut your cardboard picture into five or six jigsaw pieces.
4. Ask a classmate to put your puzzle picture together.

Name _____

 # Your Time-Machine Boat

1. In each circle, draw something you love about the world.
2. Cut out the circles and the boat.
3. Paste the circles in the boat.
4. Write your name in the blank on the boat name.

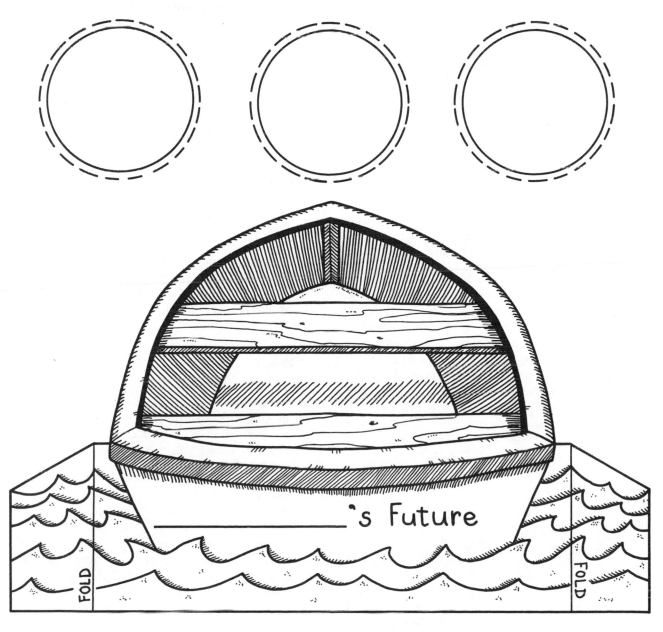

_____'s Future

FOLD

FOLD

Ox-Cart Man

Donald Hall
Illustrated by Barbara Cooney (Puffin 1983)

Summary:
A rural family in 19th-century New Hampshire uses the resources around them to produce most of what they need. In the fall, the father loads an ox-drawn cart with the "extras" and journeys to town to sell them. He uses the money to buy the tools the family needs to continue their work. As fall fades to winter and winter to spring, each member of the family carries out his or her orderly and useful tasks.

Preparation:
As you show and discuss the book cover, explain that the story tells about a farm family many years ago. Encourage students to tell what they know about things produced on farms. Point out New Hampshire on a U.S. map and ask students to listen for what this New Hampshire family produced.

As You Read
On the chalkboard, draw large outlines of a sheep, a goose, a tree, and a farm field. Direct reading by asking students to fill in the pictures with words or phrases to tell what the family gets or makes from these. (You may want to introduce the word *resource,* explaining that it means "something we use to meet our needs," and ask what need each listed item meets; for example, the sheep's wool is needed to make yarn.)

Guide reading with questions like these:
1. What special job does each person in the family have? What work does the family do together?
2. What needs does the family meet by using things they grow or raise? (food, shelter, clothing) What things does the family need that must be bought?
3. Why does the father make the long trip to town each autumn?
4. Why does the family's work change with each season?

As reading-response strategies (1.) Invite students to tell about jobs they do for their family and compare them with the work the children in the story do. (2.) Discuss why wintergreen peppermint candies are a treat for the family, and call on volunteers to tell how that treat differs from ones *they* expect. Discuss why the ox-cart man's family could not afford more expensive gifts. (3.) Encourage students to compare the outdoor market and the general store shown in the illustrations with the stores they are used to. (4.) Ask students how they feel when the father sells the ox, and how the father seems to feel and why he makes this sale. Invite students to point out illustrations that show that an ox will be available for the next autumn's trip to town.

Extending Geography Skills:
Resource Chains
1. **Vegetable Voyages**   Through a fieldtrip to a greengrocer or to the fresh-produce section of a supermarket, students can find out from the manager what fresh fruits and vegetables are produced locally, when they are in season, and which ones are shipped in from other areas of the country, or from other countries. Back in the classroom, display a large outline map of the relevant regions (e.g., the United States and Central and South America) and invite students to fill it in with pictures of fruits and vegetables that come from those areas to their local markets. Discuss why the Ox-Cart Man's family

did not have access to these resources, and why *we* do.

2. ***Lunch Links***   Students can work in groups of four to make diagrams that trace their own lunch and snack items, such as apples, bread, peanut butter, and potato chips, to their source. After groups decide on the item to be investigated, they can assign roles: two members to do research and report to the group; one member to draw pictures for the diagram; one member to write labels or captions. Invite groups to show and tell about their diagrams just before and after a school meal. Display the diagrams around the room. Discuss how getting a product such as an apple from "producer" to "eater" has changed from the days of the ox-cart man and his family.

Making Connections

Literature

1. ***Do-It Dramas***   Invite student partners to choose an illustration in the book to act out in pantomime for classmates to guess. Encourage respondents to tell not only what the action is (e.g. shearing sheep), but also (1.) *what* resource or resources are being used (e.g., wool), and (2.) why the family is using this resource (e.g., to make yarn for clothing to wear or sell).

2. ***Story Extensions***   Brainstorm a list of ways to add to the story, such as making up a conversation between two of the characters, writing and illustrating some pages to tell what the ox-cart family does in the summer, or re-telling the story to set it in today's world. Invite interested students to work independently or with a partner to extend the story and present it to the class.

Social Studies:

Seasonal Why's   Through a field trip to a farm, students can investigate how farmers today organize their tasks around seasonal considerations, just as did the long-ago farmers described in the story. You might divide the class into groups of four (one for each season) and ask each group to pay special attention to what the farmer-interviewee does in that season and why he or she must do it then. Develop a bulletin board display based on the class trip: (1.) your drawing at the center of a farm family; (2.) four spokes from the center to the labels *Winter, Spring, Summer, Fall*; (3.) under each label, the groups' pictures and sentences describing the seasonal farm work.

Art:

Panorama Pictures   Invite students to choose an illustration in the book and then make a picture showing how a modern family might work toward the same goal. For example, the picture of the woman at the loom and her daughter sewing suggests buying from bolts of fabric, using a sewing machine, or shopping for clothes in a department store. Display the finished pictures around the room in a sequence that approximately follows the sequence in the book. Suggest that students tell about their pictures by imagining that they are taking the boy and girl in the book on a tour of today's world.

Creative Writing:

Sequence Poems   Reread the paragraphs in the story that are like catalogue poems which—line by line—add details that work back to an original resource. For example:

"He packed five pairs of *mittens*
  his daughter *knit*
  from *yarn* spun at the spinning wheel
  from *sheep* sheared in April."

Invite students to compose orally lines for a group catalogue poem tracing an ordinary product back to its source. Copy the poem on the chalkboard or on poster paper. Example:

· I ate an *apple*
  That was bought at a *store*
· That got it by *truck*
  From a *farmer* who works
  To grow *apple trees*.

Suggest that students copy and illustrate the group poem and take their work home to share with their families.

Ox-Cart Trips

1. Color the things the ox pulls to town.
2. Make up a game to play with your picture. You can use buttons or coins as markers.

Start

Stuck in the mud!

Time for a nap!

End

Ox-Card Notes

1. Finish the postcard picture to show what the ox sees in town.
2. Finish the postcard note.
3. Cut out your picture and note. Paste the note on the back of the picture to make a postcard.

Greetings from
Portsmouth
New Hampshire

Dear Baby Ox,

_____

_____

_____

_____

Love,
Mama Ox

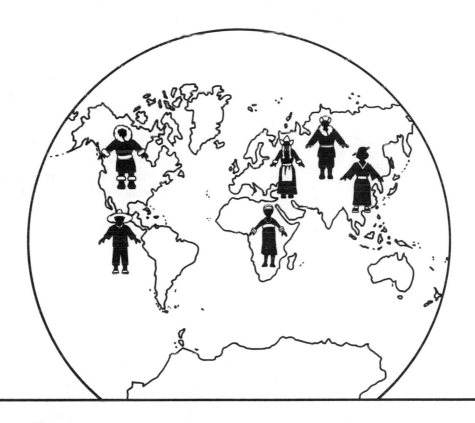

 **Story Book Level**

The Legend of the Bluebonnet

Tomie DePaola (Putnam's 1983)

Summary:

In this retelling of a Comanche legend, She-Who-Is-Alone—a little girl who has lost her family in the drought and famine afflicting her people—understands that the Great Spirit will only send rain when something of great value is sacrificed in return for all that humans have taken from Earth. The girl sacrifices her most valued possession, a doll. Her sacrifice is acknowledged as the rain falls and as new, blue flowers blossom across the parched earth.

Preparation:

On an outline map of the United States, circle the Southwestern states and explain that the story takes place long ago in Texas, a state in this region. Point out the bluebonnets on the book cover and explain that they are the state flower of Texas. Invite students to predict what the story tells about.

As You Read

To help students trace the heroine's feelings as the story progresses, invite them to fill in a chalkboard character chart at key points in the story. Encourage students to use the chart as they review or retell the story.

Situation	What She-Who-Is-Alone Feels
drought and famine	hunger, thirst
family dies	sadness, loneliness
plays with doll	love, comfort
shaman gives advice	responsibility, sadness

She-Who-Is-Alone's sacrifice of her doll affects many children very deeply. As students respond to it, encourage them to discuss what is sad about it, how the girl's action contrasts with the response of the warrior who will not give up his bow and the woman who will not give up her blanket, and how the heroine is rewarded. Invite volunteers to tell about their favorite possession and what circumstances might lead them to give it up. Discuss how a choice that a story character makes sometimes leads to both sadness and joy.

One way to review the story is to guide students to consider what makes it a *legend*. Draw an idea-web like the one below and invite students to fill in the circles with details from the story.

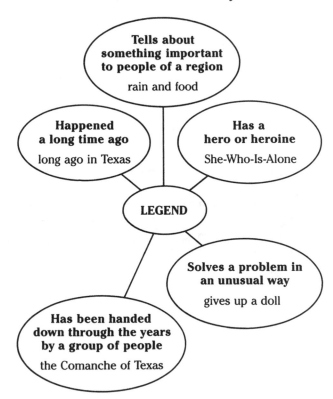

Tells about something important to people of a region — rain and food

Happened a long time ago — long ago in Texas

Has a hero or heroine — She-Who-Is-Alone

LEGEND

Solves a problem in an unusual way — gives up a doll

Has been handed down through the years by a group of people — the Comanche of Texas

Extending Geography Skills: Local Legends

On an outline map of the United States, circle and label major regions of the country (Northeast, Southeast, Midwest, Southwest, West Coast, Northwest). Invite cooperative learning groups of four or five to use the library to find an American legend of any of the regions to present to the class.

After the group has chosen a tale, they can confer to decide on the form their presentation will take (for example, an illustrated retelling, a picture-strip, a play, or a Reader's Theater format), then assign roles to each group member. Suggest that groups introduce their legends by pointing on the map to the region from which it comes. You might wish to ask the audience to listen for the features, shown in the idea-web above, that make the story a legend. After a class run-through, groups might enjoy presenting their legends to another class or to visiting families.

Making Connections

Social Studies:

State Symbols   On spokes emanating from an outline map of your state, place labels naming the official state flower, tree, and bird. (Some states also have "official" fish or insects or mammals, whose pictures you might want to add to the display or you may have students brainstorm to create their own "official" state symbols.) Invite students to find or create pictures and descriptions of the items and make their own drawings and captions to display under the labels. Suggest that students tell or write their own legends about why these plants and animals are important in the state. To culminate the activity, you might ask a community-resource person involved in forestry or environmental concerns to speak to the class about where in the state the plants and animals can currently be found. A class field trip might be organized to spot and study them.

Literature/Language:

What's In a Name?   After reviewing why the heroine's name was changed from She-Who-Is-Alone to One-Who-Dearly-Loved-Her-People, discuss how the names describe the character and the change she underwent. Invite interested students to make up an old and a new descriptive name for themselves based on a change in their own behavior or ideas. Students can draw a picture to illustrate each name. To share their work, students might discuss it with a partner, keep it in their own Story-Idea folder, or contribute it to a class Guess-Who-I-Am book to place on a reading table.

Civics:

Give-and-Take   After reviewing the shaman's idea that people are responsible for giving things back to Earth, invite students to complete a chalkboard word-and-pictures chart showing that many people today are attempting to do this. Chart pictures might include a tree, a lake or ocean, and a sunny sky. Students can make copies of the completed chart, circle the actions they or their families already carry out, and take the chart home for display.

What We Get	How We Give Back
Lumber paper fruits oxygen BEAUTY	recycle paper plant a tree protect forests use regular plates, not paper plates

Name _____

Hooray for Our State

Make up some symbols for your state. First, draw a picture to go with each label. Then, on the lines, tell why this is a good symbol for your state. Cut along the lines. Use your symbols and make up a voting game to play with your classmates.

My idea for a State food:

_____

_____

My idea for a State building:

_____

_____

My idea for a State hat:

_____

_____

My idea for a State sport:

_____

_____

Name _____

Make a newspaper story about She-Who-Is-Alone. Write the story on the lines at the left. Draw a picture and write a caption on the right.

ASHES TURN INTO FLOWERS!

_____

_____

_____

_____

_____

_____

_____

_____

_____

_____

_____

_____

_____

_____

_____

_____

Bringing the Rain to Kapiti Plain

Verna Aardema
Illustrated by Beatriz Vidal (Dial 1981)

Summary:

Though rainclouds hover, the rain doesn't fall. The young herder, Ki-pat, watches the land dry up and his cattle and other animals go thirsty. Arming an arrow with an eagle-feather, Ki-pat shoots the arrow into the cloud, and the welcome rain comes at last. This old tale from Kenya is retold with a rhythm and cumulative refrain like those in the poem "The House That Jack Built."

Preparation:

1. You may wish to write on the chalkboard lines from the story for students to say chorally as you read. (See "As You Read")
2. Establish the story locale by pointing out Kenya on a globe or on a map of Africa. Explain that a *plain* is flat stretch of land. Invite students to tell what happens to land if the rain doesn't fall.

As You Read

To build appreciation for the fun of repetition and rhythm, invite six choral reading groups of three or four students to say the lines assigned to them as you come to those lines in the story-poem and point to the choral-reading group.

Ki-pat, whose cows were so hungry and dry,	**Group 1**
They mooed for the rain to fall from the sky;	**Group 2**
To green-up the grass, all brown and dead,	**Group 3**
That needed the rain from the cloud overhead—	**Group 4**
The big, black cloud, all heavy with rain,	**Group 5**
That shadowed the ground on Kapiti Plain.	**Group 6**

Guided reading questions might focus on (1.) the kinds of animals that live on Kapiti Plain; (2.) which animals are wild and which kind is domesticated (the cattle); (3.) why Ki-pat feels such concern for the cattle (He and his people depend upon cattle for milk, meat, leather, and so forth; Ki-pat's job is to care for the cattle; being domesticated, the cattle won't wander away in search of water as the wild animals do); (4.) how the plain changes after the rains come.

Questions like the following can help you elicit students' personal responses to the story: (1.) How do you feel when your land needs rain and a raincloud above just won't burst open? (2.) What part of this story seems like real-life? What part seems like make-believe? (Can an eagle-feather on an arrow really bring rain?) (3.) Why is an eagle—unlike, say, a chicken or a robin—a good symbol for rain? (Eagles are powerful, and fly high in the sky where the rainclouds are.) (4.) What story do you think Ki-pat tells his son about how to bring rain to Kapiti Plain?

Extending Geography Skills: Climate Of Our Region

At the center of the board, place the words Climate in the (your region). On four spokes from the center, place the words Spring, Summer, Winter, Fall. Explain that *climate* means the usual kind of weather a region has at each season. Ask why Ki-pat waited so earnestly for rain. (Rainfall is scarce in all seasons on the plains of Kenya.) Invite four cooperative learning groups to choose a season, discuss the kind of weather and weather-related events expected in your region during that season, and then assign roles for making pictures and writing accompanying poems about the season to read chorally, using the book poem as a model. After groups have shared their pictures and poems with the class, post the finished work under the bulletin board labels. You may wish to record the groups' choral readings on tape for students to listen to and discuss with a partner.

These are the leaves
all yellow and brown
That fall on houses
around the town,
That children like to
put in a heap,
And shout and scatter
and jump and leap.

Science:

Keeping Weather Records On poster paper, draw a calendar for this month, with space below each date for students to record facts about *temperature, wind,* and *moisture.* Invite volunteers to choose a day and collect and record the data through observation and by listening to local radio and TV weather reports. To build the concept that weather varies while climate is relatively constant, invite students to circle the days in which the reported weather conditions are expected during this month. Invite interested students to write and share a Weather Log to trace Ki-pat's experience.

Monday	Tuesday	Wednesday
Grass is getting brown. Sun is hot.	Cattle are thirsty. Cloud but no rain.	No rain yet. Wild animals are leaving. Cattle are mooing for water.

Listening/Science:

Being a Raindrop Ask students to close their eyes and use their imaginations as you tell a story about how a raindrop forms and reaches Ki-pat's plain. Embellish the story-summary below with details of your own. When you finish, invite students to draw pictures to show their own ideas about how the story concludes.

You are a tiny speck of dust, stuck on a leaf on a tree on the Kapiti Plain. Everything around you is dry—the land, the plants, the holes that used to be filled with water. You can hear the cattle mooing for water.

Here comes a dry wind! It blows you off your leaf and sends you high into the sky. You feel light as an eagle feather! Down below, you can see Ki-pat looking up at the sky, hoping for rain for the thirsty cattle.

Wow! Now things are getting bumpy! The wind has blown you into a cloud filled with millions of other specks of dust, and you are all bumping into one another. And you are getting wet, too! The cloud has water vapor in it, and the water is covering you and turning you into a raindrop! This cloud is getting very heavy and gray with you and all the other raindrops. Ki-pat is down there, looking up at the big, gray, heavy cloud, and scratching his head with worry, and hoping for rain.

Ouch! Ki-pat shoots his arrow right toward you into the cloud! Does the arrow do the trick, or is it that the cloud is so heavy with you and the other raindrops that you start to fall? Back to Kapiti Plain you go, surrounded by millions of other raindrops.

Literature/Creative Writing:

Comparing Story Heroes If your students have read other stories or poems featuring heroes who have helped their land or people (for example, She-Who-Is-Alone in *The Legend of the Bluebonnets*), invite them to enact or draw story-strips in which the heroes meet and tell one another about their experiences. Suggest that the class watch the skits or study the stories to find out how the heroes are alike and how they are different. Likenesses and differences can be listed on a two-column chart. Invite interested students to write their own stories about heroes, referring to the "alike" column for ideas. Encourage students to think of real-life people they know or have heard about who are like the heroes in stories.

Name _____

Weather Symbols

Here are two weather symbols:

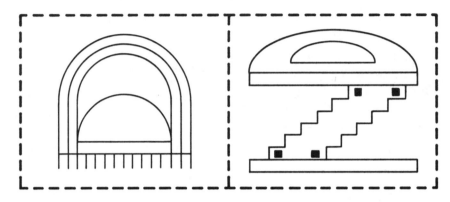

1. In the rectangles draw symbols for snow, wind, cold, and hot, clear, and cloudy.
2. Cut out all the symbols.
3. On the back of each symbol, write what it stands for.
4. Use the symbols to make an ask-and-answer weather report game.

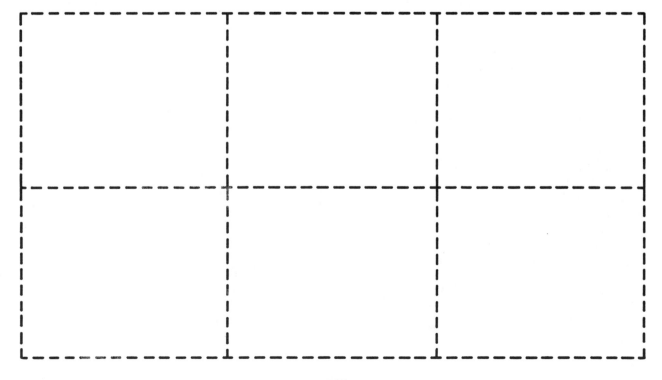

Poetry Pictures

1. Finish the lines to make a story-poem.
2. Draw pictures to go with your story-poem.
3. Cut and fold.
4. On the back of the top fold, write a title for your story.

This is the _____

that _____

that _____

Fold
2

Fold
1

Hill of Fire

Thomas P. Lewis
Illustrated by Joan Sandin (Harper 1971)

Summary:

The story is based on the eruption on February 20, 1943, of the Paricutin volcano, in the Mexican state of Michoacan. The eruption began in the cornfield of a Tarascan Indian named Dionisio Pulido. In this story, the farmer—bored by the routine in his village—constantly complains that "Nothing ever happens." Then suddenly the volcano erupts! No one is killed, but 2000 people lose their homes and have to build a new village some distance away. Though tourists flock to see the volcano, the farmer is happy to settle down into the peaceful routine he used to complain about.

Preparation:

As students study the cover and the title, explain that the "hill of fire" is a volcano, and point out Mexico—the site of this volcano—on a map. Discuss students' ideas about volcanoes. On the chalkboard, list their questions about volcanoes and invite them to listen to the story to find answers to some.

As You Read

Help students link the farmer's feelings to changing situations and events by drawing a feeling-graph on the chalkboard and inviting students to tell when the farmer had these feelings. Encourage students to use the feeling words as they discuss and retell the story.

Use questions like the following to elicit students' personal responses: (1.) Why is the farmer bored? Do you ever say "Nothing ever happens?" What kinds of things would you like to see happen? (2.) Does Pablo, the farmer's son, seem bored? What kinds of things make him happy? (3.) How does the farmer's life change when the volcano erupts? (4.) If you lived in this village, what is the first thing you would try to save? Why? (5.) Why do the villagers call the volcano *El Monstruo* (The Monster)? What other name would you give it?

Extending Geography Skills:
Inside the Earth

To help students understand the composition of Earth and the source of volcanoes, place a labeled cross-section drawing like the one below at the center of the bulletin board. As you discuss the cross-section, point out that the crust of the Earth is comparatively thin, that here and there at the bottom of the crust are pockets of melted rock, and that a volcano, a "hill of fire," is formed when this melted rock pushes up and flows out.

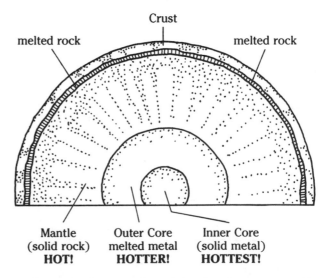

Then distribute copies of the drawing on page 43. Allow space at the bottom and top for students to

42

write. Explain that it is a cross-section of Earth's crust showing the Mexican farmer plowing his field. Invite students to use the previous discussion to tell about what is happening in the picture. Suggest that students then write their descriptions on this cross-section, color it, and add words in dialogue-balloons for the farmer and his son. Post the students' work on the bulletin board around the central picture.

Making Connections

Oral Language:
Volcano News Flash Invite cooperative learning groups of four or five to plan and present TV news shows about the eruption of El Monstruo. Roles can include (1.) an on-the-spot reporter describing the eruption as it happens; (2.) a studio reporter pointing out the location on a map; (3.) the farmer and his son being interviewed by a reporter; (4.) a program director to introduce the show and announce the different segments (e.g., "And now, back to you, Janice, at the scene of this tremendous Hill of Fire!"). Allow time for each group to practice its presentation before sharing it with the class. Conclude the activity with a general discussion in which students critique their own group's performance, telling what they like best about it and what they might want to change.

Civics:
Responsibilities Invite students to tell about situations in which their families or neighbors had to respond to an emergency caused by a natural force, such as a wind storm, blizzard, flash flood, or earthquake. Discuss people's reactions and what they did to help themselves and their neighbors. Some students might enjoy writing and illustrating an account of the incident. Suggest that they refer to the feeling-graph (above) they made for *Hill of Fire* to get ideas about how to structure their stories. Put the finished stories in a reading-table folder labeled *Emergency!* Invite students to read and discuss the stories with a partner.

Science:
Rock Hounds Review page 38 in the story, which describes the *lava* coming out of the Hill of Fire. Use the bulletin-board diagrams to point out that *lava* is the name for the melted rock that shoots and flows out of the volcano, that when the lava cools and hardens on Earth's surface it is called *igneous* rock ("igneous" means "of fire"), and that eventually soil forms and plants grow on it. Invite partners to research and report on common kinds of igneous rocks and their uses, such as granite (used for buildings and curbstones), basalt (used in building roads), pumice (ground up in household scouring powders), and obsidian (used decoratively and in jewelry). If possible, invite a geologist, quarry-miner, stone mason, or natural history museum staffer to bring samples of igneous rocks to show to the class and then lead a field trip to find and identify some of these and others kinds of rocks (metamorphic and sedimentary). Encourage interested students to collect and label different kinds of rocks and display them for the class.

Hot News

1. Color the volcano pattern below. Cut it out and fold on the fold line.
2. Use the inside of the volcano to write some hot news about what you've learned about volcanoes.

EMERGENCY NUMBERS

HOT NEWS!

VOLCANO FACTS

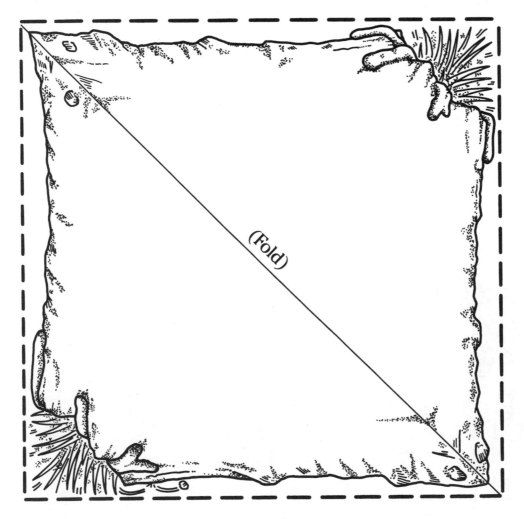

(Fold)

Name _____

Nothing Ever Happens!

1. Color the pictures and cut them out.
2. On the back of each picture, draw or write what people do when this situation occurs.
3. Use your cards to make up a game to play with a partner.

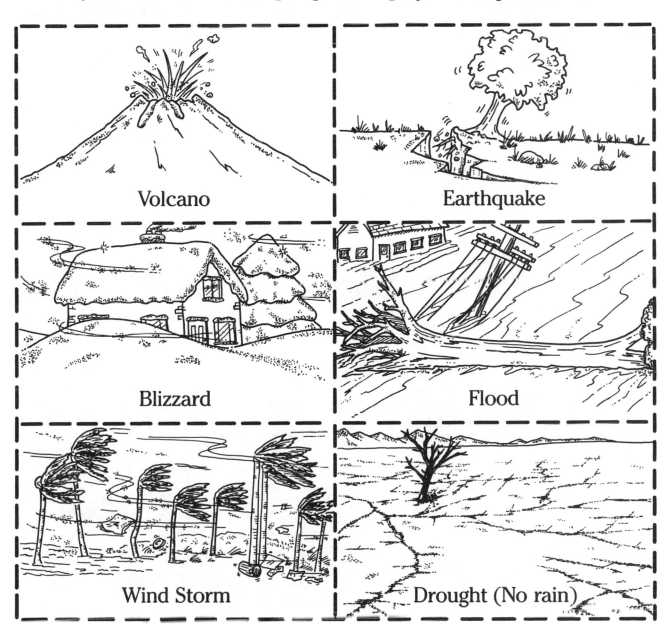

Volcano

Earthquake

Blizzard

Flood

Wind Storm

Drought (No rain)

45

I Am the Ocean

Suzanna Marshak
Illustrated by James Endicott
(Little, Brown 1991)

Summary:

The ocean speaks of the animals, large and small, who live within its waters and on its shores, and of its different aspects, from calm to stormy. The story also hints at the great age of the ocean, the rivers that feed it, and the uses humans make of it as a path.

Shore — pelicans — seagulls — crabs — jellyfish — starfish — Shallow Water — flying fish — Deep Water — whales

Preparation:

1. Make sure that students know what *ocean* means: the great body of salt water that covers three-quarters of Earth's surface. On a globe or map, point out the four main divisions of the ocean: the Atlantic, Pacific, Indian, and Arctic oceans. Invite students to tell what they know about living creatures in the ocean.

2. Invite volunteers to discuss times they have imagined they were "something else," for example, a toy, a tree, or a cloud. Explain that the book's author imagines what the ocean would talk about if it could speak.

As You Read

Invite students to fill in a chalkboard cutaway chart with names of living things mentioned in the story and shown in the illustrations. If possible, have field guides and nature encyclopedias at hand for interested students to use to find exact names of some of the animals. Use the chart later as the basis for the bulletin board activity described on page 47.

As you review or reread the pages, encourage students to listen for phrases and sentences that help them to see and hear the ocean and the life in it. Record some of the students' favorite imagery on the chalkboard or on poster paper for use later on.

Invite students to respond to the ways the ocean is made to seem like a person. For example, what moods does the ocean have? What opinion does the ocean seem to have of itself? (proud, strong). Discuss how presenting the ocean as a person is different from other presentations students have read or seen.

Extending Geography Skills:

1. **Defining Terms** Invite volunteers to use a dictionary to find and share the definitions of

lake (a body of water, larger than a pond, and surrounded by land; lake water is usually fresh, not salty) and *river* (a large stream that flows into a lake or ocean). Help students identify lakes and rivers in your area. Discuss the differences between the ocean, lakes, and rivers.

2. **Classifying Products** Organize a field trip to a supermarket with the goal of finding out what food products —fresh, canned, and frozen— come from rivers, lakes, and oceans. Enlist a market staffer as a guide who can help explain in what body of water the food product originates. Assign groups of students to be in charge of listing particular categories of food that have their source in water, such as *ocean fish, lake fish, river fish, crustaceans*. Back in the classroom, invite students to illustrate, share, and compare their lists. Discuss why so many people are concerned about the pollution of Earth's waters, and some major sources of this pollution (industrial wastes, garbage dumping, beach litterers). Invite interested students to make "Don't Dump On Me!" posters incorporating what they learned from the trip and the discussion.

Making Connections

Literature:
Words and Pictures Under the heading *I Am the Ocean,* use colored construction paper to replicate the cutaway chart shown above. Invite students to draw and cut out pictures of living things mentioned in the story, using the book illustrations and the field guides and nature encyclopedias for ideas. Then suggest that students write captions for their pictures which identify the living thing and describe it, using phrases and sentences from the book or imagery of their own. After students have shared their work with classmates, ask them to place the labelled picture on the bulletin board at the level where it belongs. If possible, take colored photos of the completed display and give a copy to each student. Suggest that students paste their photos at the top of a piece of writing paper as a lead-in to a paragraph about the ocean, then take their finished work home to share with their families.

Creative Writing:
Nature Autobiographies Brainstorm a class list of other bodies of water or landforms (such as lakes, rivers, ponds, forests, mountains, deserts) that might tell their stories as the ocean does. Then invite cooperative learning groups of four or five to choose an item from the list and write and

illustrate an *I Am . . .* book about it. Group roles might be: collecting research materials; deciding together what the speaker (the *I* in the story) will tell about; drawing or painting individual pictures; deciding together on a vivid description to go with each picture. One or two members of the group can then write the descriptions as they are dictated by the artist. Members can decide together on the order the pages will take in the book, then appoint a student to make a folder or binding. After groups have shared and discussed their work with the class, put the *I Am . . .* books on a reading table for student partners to read aloud together.

Science:
Be a Wave! To demonstrate that an ocean wave is made up of water molecules that go up and down in a circle rather than water moving forward (as a wave *seems* to do), invite students to stand as shown in the picture below:

Explain that you are going to start the wave by shaking and raising the arm of the student next to you. That student will then shake and raise the arm of the next student, and so on around the semicircle. Encourage students to keep this up until they have a smooth, rhythmic movement going. Many will have "done the wave" at a sporting event and will understand what to do. To enhance the rhythm, you may wish to play in the background one of the many available tapes of the sound of the surf. When the "wave" is moving smoothly, invite the students to keep it up as you lead them very slowly around the room. Explain that they are now a *current,* and that along with their waving movement they are showing how ocean water circulates across vast areas. Conclude the activity by inviting students to tell why the ocean is often compared to a *cradle* (slow, rocking motion; birthplace and home of life).

Up and Over

1. Draw pictures or write to show what the ocean holds. Work up from Line 1 and over to Line 5.
2. Color the wave and cut it out.

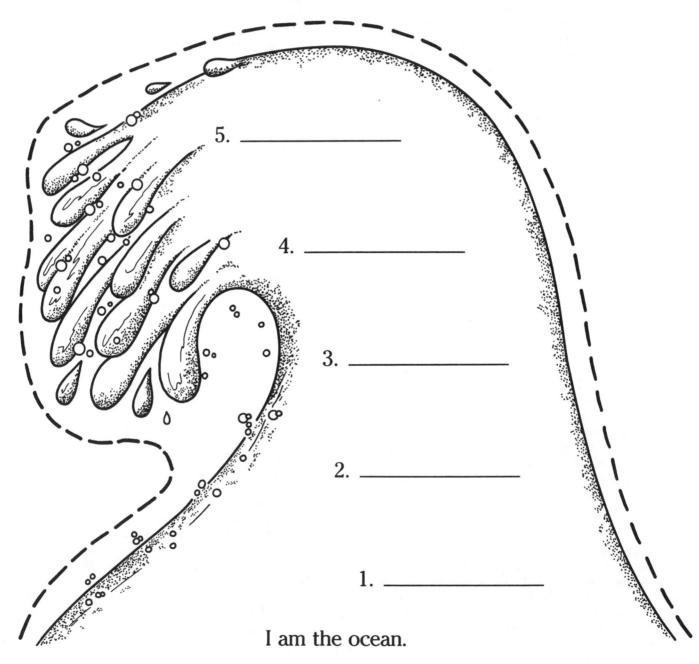

5. _____

4. _____

3. _____

2. _____

1. _____

I am the ocean.

Name _____

 **Give Us a Hand!**

1. Color us! Cut us out!
2. Bend the tabs and paste them together to make us finger puppets.
3. Use us in a play about the ocean that you write.

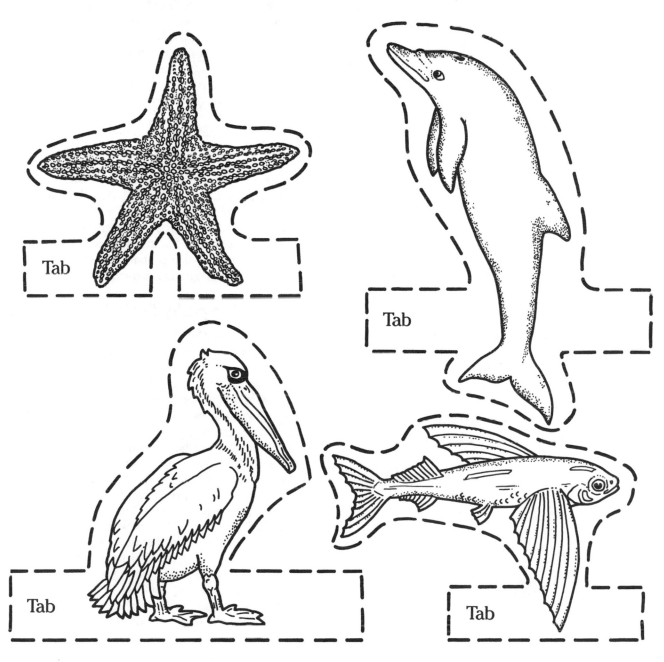

Tab

Tab

Tab

Tab

The Magic Fan

Keith Baker (Harcourt 1989)

Summary:

Yoshi makes ordinary things, until the day that he finds a magic fan. As he opens the fan, pictures are revealed to him of greater and more wonderful things he can make, such as ships, kites, and bridges. The people of the village fail to see how these inventions are useful, until the day the fan reveals that a tsunami—a giant wave—is on the way. The people save themselves by clinging to Yoshi's bridge. The magic fan is lost in the storm; the boy wonders how he will now know what to build. Looking at his own reflection in the water, Yoshi realizes that the "magic" is within *him*. He inspires his neighbors to rebuild their village, and he goes on to dream and plan more great inventions.

Preparation:

On the chalkboard, draw a cartoon "Idea Bubble" and discuss what it stands for. Invite volunteers to tell about "great ideas" they have had and how they think they got them. Show the book cover and ask students to predict how the boy in the story thinks he gets *his* ideas. Point out Japan on a map or globe to establish the story setting.

As You Read

Help students track the sequence of Yoshi's inventions and ideas by inviting them to fill in the sections in a fan you draw on the chalkboard. Discuss which ideas "reach beyond the village" and which ones help the village in the here-and-now.

Guide reading by discussing Yoshi's motivations. Some reflect his concern and love for his people. Others reflect his inventive, exploring nature. What does he build at first? (things people need in their everyday life) What does he want to build? How does the magic fan help him get ideas? Why does Yoshi start to destroy the bridge he just built? (As students consider the approaching tidal wave, you may wish to point out that Japan is an island-nation and ask students how a huge wave poses a special danger to people along the coasts.)

To help students respond to the story, focus on Yoshi as a "dreamer" and a "lone-er." What feelings do his neighbors have about the ship, the kite, and the bridge? How might Yoshi feel about their reactions? What keeps Yoshi plugging along at his inventions? How does his inventive spirit save the village? How does Yoshi probably feel when he realizes that the magic is his own?

Extending Geography Skills: People as Changers

Make individual snapshots of students and arrange them on the board under the head *Our Magic Fans*. Leave space around each photo for students to add their own dialogue fans. Invite each student to write and cut out two dialogue fans for his or her own picture: one to say what the student is doing now that fills him or her with pride, and one to tell about something the student wishes to do or make in the future. After putting the dialogue fans in place, invite the class to study the display and discuss (1.) how the "present" fans give clues to the "future" fans, and (2.) how what the student wishes to do or make in the future might contribute to the lives of other people as well. Recycle the bulletin board when you disassemble it by inviting interested students to use the photos and the information on the dialogue fans to make a class yearbook for display on a reading table.

Making Connections

Literature/Creative Writing:

Unsung Heroes   The study of Geography includes the changes that happen on the land because of people's inventions and technology. For many of the most basic inventions, no individual inventor is known. Invite the class to brainstorm a list of simple inventions that make human travel and exploration easier. You might start with two of the inventions named in the story: ships and bridges. Explain that we really do not know for sure who the individuals were that first dreamed of and made these devices. Other examples of inventions that help us go places are shoes; wheels; rafts; trail markers; sails; oars; maps.

Next, invite cooperative learning groups to choose one of the items and write and illustrate a story tracing its imagined invention. Suggest that the group as a whole plan the story plot by discussing the outset (1.) how the inventor got his or her idea, (2.) the steps leading to the invention, (3.) how the invention benefits many, many people. Then group roles can be assigned: individual members to draw and write about particular steps in the story; an editor/checker to keep the incidents in sequential order and make sure each step is clearly covered. Suggest that groups develop different ways of presenting their stories to the class. Examples are: reading the story and showing the pictures; acting the process out in a skit; displaying the pictures and text as a time line; enacting the story as a taped radio-play. The activity could culminate with a discussion of ways ordinary people are resources in real life through the human ability to invent new things and provide important new services for their neighbors.

Science/Math:

Here Comes the Wave!   A tidal wave, or *tsunami* (Japanese: "storm wave") like the one described in the story has nothing to do with true tides. Rather, it is caused by undersea earthquakes or by hurricanes far out at sea. Invite interested students to research what measurements scientists make to predict when a tidal wave or a tsunami may hit land. Suggest that students present their findings to the class by imagining that they are a grown-up Yoshi who uses modern instruments instead of a magic fan to tell neighbors why and when a tidal wave or a tsunami may hit them. Students might frame their reports as a TV weather forecaster would, using a map and pointer. Discuss with the classroom audience the ways in which people who invent measuring instruments and people who give weather forecasts are *resources,* that is, how they are useful to other people.

Thinking Skills/Art:

Models for the Future   Review the last page of the story, which names other things that Yoshi wants to invent that will reach beyond the village: "bells to talk with thunder," "nets to catch the falling stars," and "towers to watch for secrets in the sea." Invite students to imagine what such inventions might look like and to make models of them to show and explain to the class. Some students may know about modern instruments people have actually invented to help perform the tasks, such as radar, sonar, weather satellites, telescopes, and deep-space rockets. Encourage students to make models showing their ideas for other inventions that they think would improve human life. Suggest that students invite their families or other classes to view the models.

51

Name _____

A Fan Plan

1. Cut out the pattern below.

2. Fold a sheet of construction paper and put the pattern on the fold.
3. Cut around the pattern.
4. Open up your fan. Draw a picture on it of something you would like to invent. Show your magic fan to your classmates and tell about your invention.

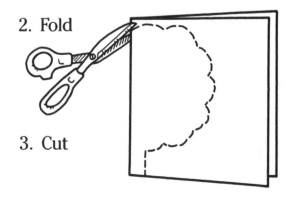

2. Fold

3. Cut

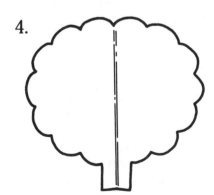

4.

Name _____

Lost and Found

Finish the Lost notice to tell about the magic fan.

Lost: One Magic Fan

Description: _____

_____

_____

_____

If you find the fan, please notify _____

_____

Finish the Found notice to tell about Yoshi.

Found: Boy With Magic In Him

Description: _____

_____

_____

If this person is something like you, please tell how. _____

_____

_____

The Drinking Gourd

F. N. Monjo
Illustrated by Fred Brenner (Harper 1970)

Summary:

Little Jeff and his family are escaping from a slave state and heading north to Canada via the Underground Railroad. The Drinking Gourd, or Big Dipper, is both a directional pointer to the north and a symbol of their freedom. Tommy Fuller's family provides a "station" along the way; Tommy's father is a "conductor" who will take Jeff's family undercover to the next leg of their journey. Tommy becomes involved in the escape plan, and in the process learns to make some hard choices.

Preparation:

1. Display a map of the United States and Canada for reference as students track the general escape route: from South Carolina, through the states north of Maryland and the Ohio River, and on across the Canadian border.
2. Point out the constellation shown on the book cover and the bright star high to the right. Suggest that students listen to find out why these stars are important.

As You Read

Use a chalkboard plot-map to guide students' understanding of how events in the story are linked. Conclude the reading of each chapter by inviting students to discuss the events and decide which ones are most important. Write a summary of their ideas in the chapter box.

Tommy is naughty in church and is sent home.	Tommy meets Jeff. Jeff tells about the Drinking Gourd.	Jeff's family hides in the hay wagon. Father heads for the river.			
1	2	3	4	5	6

As a reading-response strategy, invite students to tell what feelings the characters probably have at key points in the story. For example, how does Tommy feel when he is sent home from church? How does Jeff's family, hiding in the hay loft, feel when they hear someone moving around in the barn? Toward the end of the story, Tommy has to consider some heavy ethical questions: When, if ever, is it right to lie? to break the law? As students discuss Tommy's feelings in these situations, help them to see that he is struggling with different ideas and emotions, such as truthfulness vs. a desire to protect, and the wish to be law-abiding vs. the knowledge that some laws seem unfair and hurtful.

Extending Geography Skills: Using a Scale of Miles

To help students understand the challenging and difficult voyage Jeff and his family undertook, first organize a one-mile class hike to help develop a concept of what a mile "means." Back in the classroom, discuss the "fatigue factor" and any problems that happened along the way. Then display a United States map that includes a mile-scale and a compass rose. Invite students to use rulers or lengths of string along with the map and scale to answer and ask questions about the approximate mileage between key points, such as from the South Carolina border to the Canadian border, or from their state capital to the capital of a neighboring state. Encourage students to use directional words as they phrase and answer questions, such as "About how many miles *north* did Jeff have to travel to get from South Carolina to Canada?" Remind students that Jeff's family had to travel mostly on foot, with only occasional rides by cart, wagon, or boat; and that the trip had to be made not on major thoroughfares, but through fields and forests so as to try to avoid detection and capture. Conclude the activity by inviting students to imagine they are Jeff and tell the class how they feel after the first mile, the tenth mile, and the hundredth mile. Encourage students to explain why Jeff and his family were willing to undertake this rigorous trip by foot. Invite interested students to tell what goal might impel them to walk hundreds of miles.

Making Connections

Literature/Art:
Plots and Pictures At the center of the board place labelled pictures of Jeff and Tommy. At the ends of six spokes from the center, place Chapter labels from the Table of Contents (e.g., *Chapter One: Fishing in Church*). Invite students to choose a chapter from the chalkboard plot-map (see page 54) and draw an illustration of the chapter event. On their drawings, students can copy the summary the class devised, or write a new one of their own. Place the completed work for each chapter in a "pad" under the chapter title on the bulletin board. Suggest that student partners review and discuss the story in sequence by turning at random to a page in each pad, chapter by chapter. To recycle the activity, when you disassemble the bulletin board put the pages at random in a folder on a reading table; invite students to work with the pages to reconstruct the story in sequence.

Science:
Star-Seekers Invite cooperative learning groups of four or five students to research major constellations such as Big Bear (Ursa Major), Little Bear (Ursa Minor), Andromeda, Cassiopeia, Orion, and the Pleiaides. Groups can replicate their constellation with cut-out stars pasted on black or dark blue paper, then tell classmates who or what the star-picture shows. To initiate the activity: (1.) First review with students page 28 of the story, in which Jeff explains to Tommy how a star formation (the Big Dipper or Drinking Gourd)

enables him and his family to keep tracking North. Explain that the Drinking Gourd is a *constellation*— a group of stars that seem to form a picture in the night sky—and that for thousands of years travelers used constellations to guide them from place to place; (2.) If possible, arrange a class trip to a planetarium or invite a planetarium-staffer to visit and talk about the positions of constellations.

Using a star-map as a guide, display groups' constellation-pictures across the room in the approximate position they have at this time of year. Invite students to make up travel games in which—pretending they are Jeff—they use direction words (*north, south,* etc.) and constellation names to tell classmates how to move from one point in the classroom to another. Suggest that interested students tell their families at home the story of *The Drinking Gourd,* then ask family members to help them find the Drinking Gourd and other constellations in the real night sky.

Music:
Following a Song The first pages of the book give the words of the old song "Follow the Drinking Gourd." Among the many recordings of this song, one of the best is sung by children, on the tape "Headstart with the Child Development Group of Mississippi." (*Smithsonian Folkways,* 416 Hungerford Drive, Suite 320, Rockville, Maryland 20852. Invite students to listen to this or another recording of the song, follow along in the book, sing along with the recording, and learn some of the words by heart. Suggest that students make a tape recording of their own rendition to use as background to a play based on the story. Invite interested student-partners to compose and present their own songs about traveling toward freedom.

Name _____

Star Maps

Imagine a new constellation.
1. Draw stars under the labels north, south, east, and west.
2. Draw more stars to make a star picture in the sky. Connect your stars with lines.
3. Write the name of your new constellation.
4. Show your classmates how they could use your constellation to find their way at night.

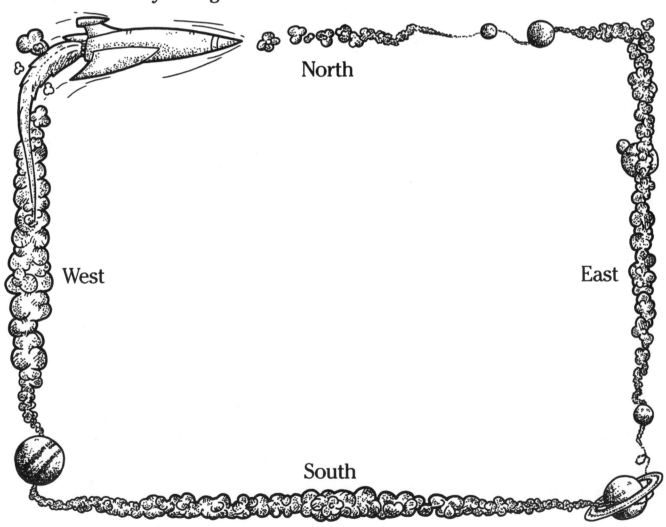

North

West

East

South

The name of my constellation is _____.

Name _____

Story Railroad

1. Write a part of a story on each railroad car.
2. Cut out each railroad car.
3. Ask a classmate to put your story in order with the engine first.

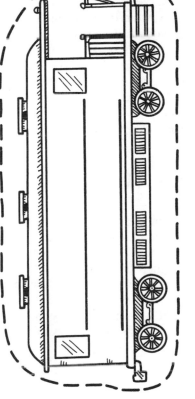

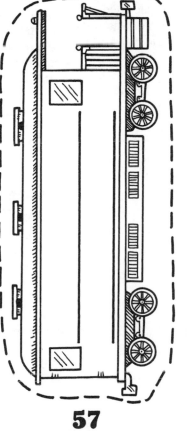

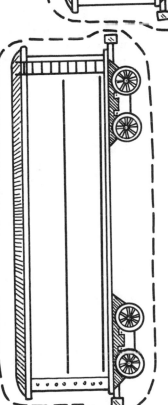

The Gift of the Sacred Dog

Paul Goble (Macmillan 1980)

Summary:

This is a legendary telling of how the nomadic buffalo-hunters of the Great Plains acquired horses. According to the legend, the people were suffering because they couldn't travel fast enough to hunt down the buffalo herds, on which they depended for food. They had only dogs to pull their travoises, and in times of drought and famine even the dogs gave out. A young boy, determined to help his people, travels to a lonely place, prays to the Great Spirit, and has a visionary dream in which "sacred dogs" (actually horses) of great speed and strength come to his people's aid. The dream comes true. The people give thanks and promise to take good care of the horses forever.

Preparation:

1. Point out the Great Plains region on a United States map. Explain that millions of buffalo used to live in the region and that Native Americans depended on them as a source of food.
2. As students discuss the cover, explain that "sacred" means "holy," or "something to be respected." Suggest that students listen to find out why a horse is called a *sacred dog*.

As You Read

Guide comprehension by discussing why the people in the story at first think that horses are a kind of larger, swifter dog. Invite students to complete a Venn diagram that shows the differences and likenesses.

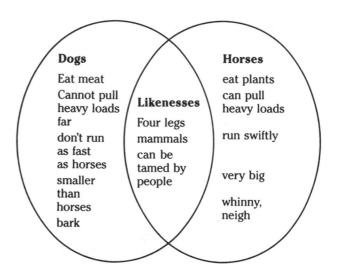

Dogs	Likenesses	Horses
Eat meat		eat plants
Cannot pull heavy loads far	Four legs	can pull heavy loads
don't run as fast as horses	mammals can be tamed by people	run swiftly
smaller than horses		very big
bark		whinny, neigh

To help students respond to the young hero's adventure, invite volunteers to tell about times they have tried to help their friends or family. What special things did they decide to do? What was difficult and what was rewarding about their undertaking? In the story, what difficult things does the boy experience? (he goes off on his own; he has a scary dream) What is his reward? (knowing that his people can now hunt the buffalo).

As you read the last pages of the story, suggest that students listen and look at the illustrations to find clues about how the people in the story feel about Earth's resources and how they act as a result.

Extending Geography Skills: Animal Resources

Invite cooperative learning groups of four or five to choose an animal, research ways in which it contributes to the environment and/or to human well-being, and present their findings to the class. You might introduce the activity by discussing the ways in which people have used horses and dogs in their work; for example, horses to pull wagons and plows and to carry riders swiftly; dogs to protect, herd sheep, guide the blind, and—as in the story—pull loads, as malamutes in the North still do. Invite students to brainstorm a list of other familiar animals, both domestic and wild, and ranging across a wide spectrum. They might start with animals shown or named in the book (such as vultures, crows, and several other kinds of birds; wolves; deer; chipmunks; butterflies, bats), then list other animals in their own environment such as earthworms, bees, mice, cats, squirrels. Each cooperative learning group can select one of the animals, then assign the roles of researchers, artists, writers, and editor-organizer. Remind the groups that the purpose is to find ways in which the animal contributes to life as a whole. (Earthworms, for instance, aereate the soil.) The group can hold a conference to decide how they wish to present their findings to the class. Possibilities are: a poster-diagram; an illustrated book; an oral report with visuals; a quiz-show format. At the end of each presentation, invite the classroom audience to tell what they learned about the animal.

Making Connections

Literature:
Being a Story Character   Invite students to imagine that they are one of the following story characters and to tell about the hero from that character's point of view: a dog who must pull a travois; a buffalo-dancer; the magic rider in the boy's dream; a "sacred dog;" a buffalo. Students can write and illustrate their responses, or work with a small group to make a tape recording in which the different characters speak. After the finished products have been shared with the class, discuss how the boy's actions affect different characters in different ways. What might have happened if the boy had not taken on the responsibility of helping his people? Invite volunteers to tell how carrying out a chore or another responsibility of their own affects the total environment.

Science:
Caring for Animals   Review how the boy's people felt responsible for the animals and plants around them. Discuss the idea of *stewardship* with the class: the concept that because human beings are *powerful* enough to change the environment in radical ways, they are also *responsible* for taking care of the plants and animals in that environment. If possible, organize a field trip to a nature center where students can find out about the needs of local wildlife and how young people can help fill these needs. Examples are: building bird nesting boxes; designing, making, and maintaining bird feeders; working with a local environmental group to green-up an area with wildlife plantings to provide food and shelter for small animals. Invite interested students to form groups to plan and carry out one of these or another stewardship project. Encourage groups to give up-date reports to the class now and then to describe their progress and what they are learning.

Creative Writing:
Poems of Praise   Read the Sioux songs about the buffalo and the horse which conclude the book. (Explain that the "nation" referred to in the first poem means the buffalo herd.) Invite the class to decide on an animal they would like to praise, then work together to compose a poem for that animal. Write the lines of the poem on the chalkboard as students develop them. Invite students to arrange the completed poem for choral reading and then say it aloud together. Students can then make and illustrate individual copies of the poem to display around the room or take home to share with their families. Invite interested students to work individually or with a partner to write poems in praise of other animals. Put the poems in a folder on a reading table for students to read and discuss.

Many Thanks!

1. Write about three things you are thankful for. Use the lines on the horses on this page.
2. Color the horses. Cut on the heavy lines.
3. Make a hole on the tab and put a string through it. Hang up your thank-you note.

Good Deeds Days

1. On each ticket, write a good deed that will help the thing or person shown in the picture.
2. Color the tickets and cut them out.
3. Find ways to trade tickets with your friends, or do good deeds together.

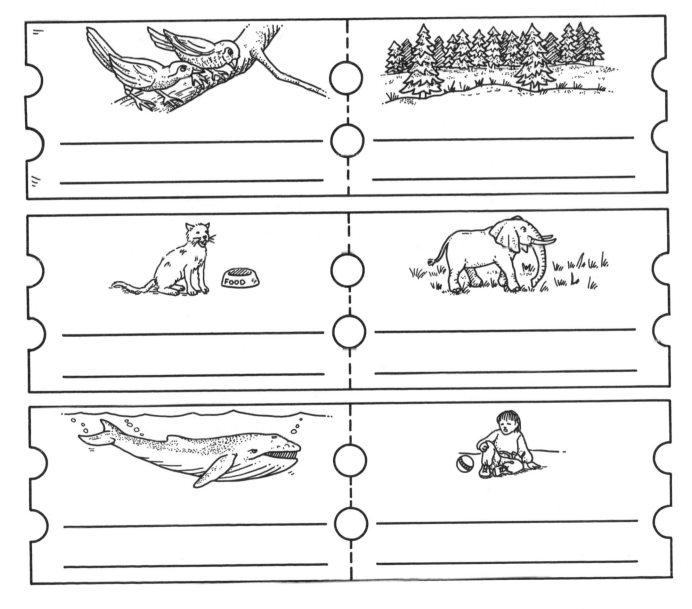

Three Names

Patricia MacLachlan
Illustrated by Alexander Pertzoff
(HarperCollins 1991)

Summary:

From his great-grandfather, the narrator learns what it was like to live and go to school on the prairie many years ago. Three Names, great-grandfather's dog, goes to the one-room schoolhouse each day with the children. Like them, he notes the changing seasons, enjoys the camaraderie of the small classroom (where pupils teach as well as learn), and spends the summer waiting eagerly for school to begin again.

Preparation:

1. Explain that the story is set long ago on a *prairie,* and that a prairie is flat or hilly land covered chiefly by tall grass. Point out on a map the North American prairie: from central Texas northward through the southern part of the Canadian province of Saskatchewan.

2. As you show the covers and preview the illustrations, invite students to predict whether the story takes place long ago or today. Encourage students to give reasons for their predictions.

As You Read

Use a chalkboard chart like the one below to guide comprehension of likenesses and differences between the great-grandfather's schooldays and those of your students.

	Then	Now
Going to school	wagon, walk, horses	bus, walk
School lunch	bring in a pail	buy, lunchbox
Outside the school	barn, outhouses	playground
Games		
Heat and water		

Encourage students to respond to the story by telling (1.) what they would like or dislike about attending a school like the one described, and (2.) what activities from great-grandfather's school days are similar to one in their own school, for example, playing with friends, having special snacks, giving holiday parties, and helping one another learn.

Extending Geography Skills: Comparing Visuals

On the left side of the board, display a topographical map of the Prairie states under the heading *The Prairie From Up High.* After discussing what the map tells about the altitude, land forms, water bodies, and so forth of this region, explain to students that a topographical map shows a "bird's eye view" of a region. Invite students to review with you the story and the illustrations to get an up-close view, or Three Name's "dog's-eye view," of the same region. As students discuss the pictures and note descriptive phrases, write their observations on the chalkboard (for example, "flat land," "ponds (sloughs)," "prairie grass, wheat, paintbrush, bluegrass," "cold winters"). Distribute strips of paper and suggest that students choose and illustrate some of the chalkboard phrases. Place the strips to the right of the map under the heading *The Prairie Up Close.* Extend the activity by inviting students to suggest how the prairie has changed since great-grandfather's day (growth of cities, building of highways, more people, etc.). Some students may enjoy writing a description or drawing and captioning a picture that tells what a modern-day Three Names might see if he were on his way to school on the prairie today. Place the descriptions and drawings in a folder near the bulletin board for students to read and discuss independently.

Making Connections

Creative Writing

1. *Geography Poems*   Reread the poem which a child in great-grandfather's school wrote about the prairie. After discussing what the poem tells about a sky-scene on the prairie, invite students to write their own poems about a sky or land scene in their own region. Students can illustrate their poems and display them around the room.

2. *Canine Characters*   Invite students to make picture panels with dialogue balloons that (1.) tell the book story from Three Name's point of view, or (2.) recount the adventures of one of their own household pets, should it come to school with them. After students have shown and read their picture panels to the class, discuss what is the same and what is different about the pets' adventures and observations at a long-ago school and at a modern one. Invite pairs of students to enact a conversation between Three Names and a "today-pet," using the picture panels for ideas.

Science:

Tornado Time   Review page 26 of the story, which tells about a tornado and its effects. Invite interested students to research tornadoes to find out how they are formed and where they usually occur. After students have presented their findings to the class, discuss "threatening" weather that typically occurs in your region (e.g., blizzards, hurricanes, rainstorms) and how people today try to protect themselves—as the students in the story do—in these situations.

Social Studies:

Each One Teach One   Discuss why a one-room schoolhouse was sufficient for many communities in great-grandfather's time (smaller population). After reviewing the ways in which older students in one-room schoolhouses helped younger students (pages 18–19), invite cooperative learning groups of five or six to decide what skill they could teach to students in the grades below theirs, and what they would like to learn from students in the higher grades. Group roles might include: two members to request a group visiting-time to the lower and upper-grade classrooms; two members to plan the way the group will teach a skill to younger children; two members to list the group's reactions to the teach-and-learn sessions and report about them to the class. Suggest various forms for the reports, such as two-column charts listing what was difficult and what was easy; picture-panels showing highlights of the visits; informal skits enacting humorous moments; taped interviews with the students in the upper and lower grades who participated in this activity to get *their* reactions to it. As a concluding discussion, invite students to tell about ways in which they—like the children in great-grandfather's schoolhouse—both teach and learn within their own classroom every day.

A Prairie Long Ago

1. Cut out the pictures at the bottom that show what Three Names saw.
2. Paste the pictures on the map. Use your map to tell about three names.

Name _____

Slates and Snacks

On the slate, write something that both you and great-grandfather learn in school. In the pail, draw something that both you and great-grandfather might eat at school.

Molly's Pilgrim

Barbara Cohen
Illustrated by Michael J. Deraney
(William Morrow 1983)

Summary:

Molly and her family are Russian Jews, recently immigrated to the United States. In the small town where they finally settle, Molly endures the taunts of classmates who are not used to newcomers. When the teacher assigns students to make clothespin dolls representing Pilgrims for a Thanksgiving display, Molly's troubles seem to increase: the doll her mother makes for her shows not the typical Pilgrim, but a Russian woman dressed much like Mother herself. Mother explains that this is appropriate, for she, too, is a pilgrim: one who travels to another land in search of religious freedom. Molly's classmates make fun of her doll, until Molly explains it and her teacher backs her up by describing the Jewish harvest holiday on which the American Pilgrims based the first Thanksgiving.

Preparation:

Invite students to tell what they think a pilgrim is. Definitions at this stage will probably be far-ranging. Write them on the chalkboard, for revision after students have read the book.

As You Read

Help students use a globe to locate Russia and the United States. Invite volunteers to use a length of string to mark a route westward from Russia to America and to name some of the countries and the ocean that Molly and her parents had to cross in their journey. Explain that in those days before airplanes, immigrants traveled by land, then by ship, in voyages that might take several months.

Use questions like the following to encourage students to repond to the conflicts that Molly faces:

1. What problems does Molly face at school? Why does Elizabeth tease her? How does it feel to be teased?

2. Why doesn't Molly want her mother to come to school? How does Molly learn that she was mistaken to be embarrassed about her mother?

3. What do the pictures tell about the time when the story takes place? Do problems like Molly's take place in classrooms today, too? Why?

4. What do Molly's classmates learn about Pilgrims by the end of the story? Why does their attitude toward Molly change?

Extending Geography Skills: Comparing A Globe And A Map

Display a world map on a wall above your globe. Explain that the globe is a map that has been printed on a hollow sphere, and that it gives a truer picture of Earth and its land and water than a map because its surface is rounded like the Earth's surface is. Then ask students to identify the main way in which a world map is different from a globe (a map is flat). Invite a volunteer to locate Russia and the United States on the globe again, then find them on the map.

To help students understand that flat maps are not as accurate in their portrayal of the area of land and oceans as globes are, direct attention to the North and South polar regions, especially Greenland, on the globe, and ask students to find these regions on the flat map and encourage them to tell about the size-difference between them. Invite students to suggest why people nevertheless make and use maps (for general reference; to show small areas up close; to show the location of towns, cities, and highways; to show national boundaries; to show mountains, hills, and flat areas). If possible, assemble a collection of different kinds of maps for students to study and discuss.

Invite students whose families have recently come to the United States from other countries to flag the countries with sticker-labels on both the globe and the flat map, beginning with Russia—Molly's original home.

Making Connections

Language:
What Does It Mean?   In the story, Mama uses various Yiddish words and expressions. First, ask students to guess what the words might mean in the context of the sentence in which they are used. Then provide the English translations:

shaynkeit = beautiful
Malkeleh = Little Queen. (The name "Molly" is derived from it.)
paskudnyaks = rascals
nu – so, well

Invite students who speak other languages at home to contribute words and expressions and their meanings to a class list of *Wonderful Words*. Post the list and encourage students to learn and use some of the expressions and words that are new to them.

Literature:
Dramatic Retelling   Discuss the three basic problems Molly faces: how to cope with her treatment by her classmates; how to explain to her mother what the assignment is at school and why the doll doesn't seem to meet the description given in the assignment; how to explain the doll to her classmates and teacher. Invite three cooperative learning groups to select one of the problems and plan a skit to act it out. One group member can note the sequence of actions the group decides on. The group as a whole can assign roles in the skit. One or two members can organize and direct a brief rehearsal. Invite the groups to present their skits in the story sequence. Tape-record the skits for students to listen to, to make sure all the important incidents are there. Add to the tape, if necessary, with narrative to connect the incidents. Invite student partners to listen to the finished tape as they review the story and look at the pictures.

Social Studies:
Modern-Day Pilgrims   Encourage students to relate the story to current news about immigrants (pilgrims) from other countries, such as Vietnam, Korea, Haiti, Cuba, Cambodia, and Guatemala. Discuss what freedoms or opportunities the modern-day pilgrims are seeking in their new home. If possible, ask students to interview a newly-arrived pilgrim to find out when the pilgrim came, where he or she came from, what he or she was looking for, and what problems had to be faced on arrival. Encourage interviewers to make notes and compile them into an oral presentation for the class. The presenter should also indicate on a globe or map the country from which the pilgrim came.

Art:
Doll Maps   Invite students to make clothespin dolls dressed in the traditional clothing of their ethnic group. Display a large map of the world in the center of the bulletin board, and mount the dolls around it. Use colored yarn to connect each doll to the country it represents.

Civics:
Welcome Packages   Ask the class to imagine that a student from another country will soon enter their classroom. Discuss and list what the new classmate might want to know about the school and neighborhood (e.g., location of school rooms; holidays celebrated at school; names of playground games and their rules; names of school personnel; location of key landmarks in the school neighborhood, such as bus stops and stores). Suggest that students choose items from the list and make enclosures for a Welcome Package, such as maps, lists, descriptions, and pictures. Invite student partners to act out a meeting with a newcomer to show a way to make the newcomer feel welcome. If there is no immediate way to use the Welcome Package in your classroom, implement the final product by suggesting that students present it to another neighborhood newcomer.

Thinking Skills:
Media Contrasts   *Molly's Pilgrim* is retold in a video which won the 1985 Academy Award for best-live action short (24 minutes). It is available on a cassette from Phoenix Films. After showing the film, discuss how it is different from the book (set in modern times; new characters; some new scenes). Encourage students to tell what they would add or subtract from the story if they were the film director.

Molly's Worlds

1. In Circle 1, draw a picture to show why Molly's family left Russia.
2. In Circle 2, draw a picture to show what happened to Molly in the United States.
3. Draw an arrow between the circles to show the direction Molly's family traveled. Use your map-picture to tell Molly's story to your friends or family.

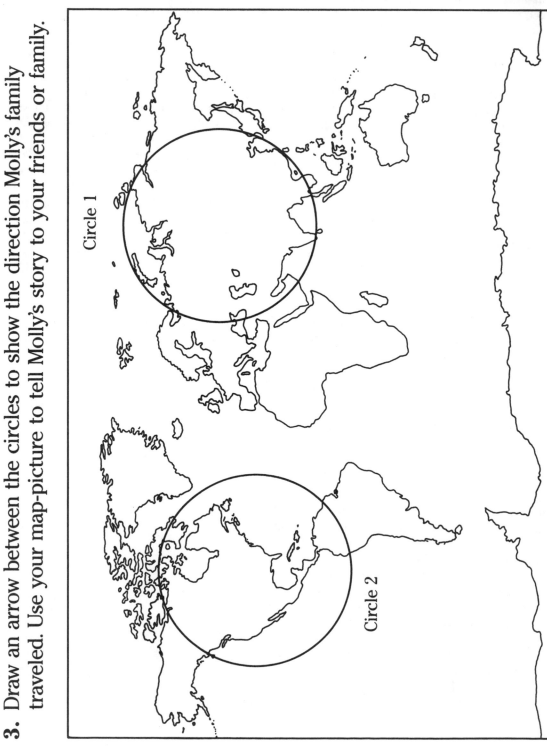

Circle 1

Circle 2

Pilgrim Puppets

1. Color the two pilgrim puppets.
2. In the empty outline, draw your idea for a pilgrim puppet.
3. Paste the pilgrim puppets on cardboard and cut them out. Use your puppets to act out a story about coming to the United States, or about Thanksgiving.

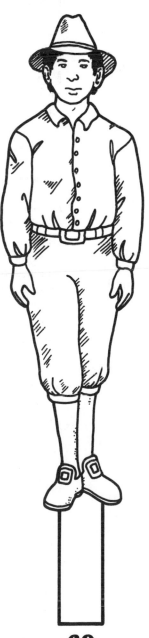
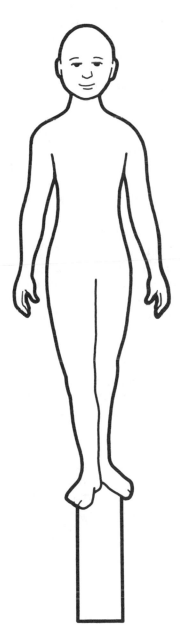

Chin Chiang and the Dragon's Dance

Ian Wallace (Atheneum 1984)

Summary:

Chin Chiang and his family live in a Chinese community within a large North American city. As people of the community prepare for their New Year's celebration, the boy dreads more and more his promise to help his grandfather carry the great, festive dragon in the parade. Chin Chiang considers himself clumsy, and fears he will stumble as he does the dragon's dance. He runs away to hide in the library, where he meets an elderly woman, Pu Yee. She knows the Dragon's Dance from long ago, and teaches it to Chin Chiang. The two return to the parade site. The boy hopes Pu Yee will take his place, but his Grandfather spots him and insists he take up his position at the dragon's tail. The boy, fearful at first, soon does the steps Pu Yee taught him, as his neighbors cheer the wonderful dance of the dragon.

Preparation:

1. Point out China on a map or globe. Explain that the first Chinese settlers came to North America more than a hundred years ago. Point out the west coasts of the United States and Canada as you explain that many Chinese settled in cities of that region.
2. Show the book jacket or another illustration of the dragon, and explain that in China the dragon is a symbol of good luck.

As You Read

To **guide** students' reading, suggest they examine the illustrations to find details that tell about the Chinese community and details that show this community is part of a larger city in North America (English-language signs, styles of buildings). Point out the mountains shown in several of the pictures, and call attention to Mrs. Lau's wish that the nets will be full of fish in the New Year. Invite students to use these clues along with the map to tell where Chin Chiang's city is (in a mountainous region along the coast).

As students discuss Chin Chiang's reluctance to do the dragon's dance, help them **respond** to his situation by asking about times they have been afraid to do something their families and friends expected of them. How does it feel to be pressured? Do students think Chin Chiang would have been able to do the dance without the help of Pu Yee?

Extending Geography Skills: Exploring Neighborhoods

At the center of the board, display a map of your city or of a large city near you. Explain that when people from other countries come to a new country, they usually bring many of their customs with them. In this way, cities grow not only in population, but also in appearance and availability of different resources and ideas. Invite students to give examples based on trips they have made through the city (e.g., stores or restaurants where ethnic foods are available; different styles of dressing; parades and festivals celebrating ethnic holidays; different languages heard on the streets or seen on signs). Arrange brief walking tours—perhaps guided by a student or another knowledgeable resident—through two or three ethnic neighborhoods and ask students to look for similarities and differences among them. Back in the classroom, invite students to draw and caption pictures showing what impressed them most or what they liked best in the various neighborhoods. Post the pictures around the city map and suggest that students study, read, and discuss them with a classmate.

Making Connections

Social Studies:
Let's Celebrate!   Review what the story tells and shows about the elements of the Chinese New Year celebration and write ideas on the chalkboard (lanterns shaped like animals, parades, special foods, dancing, music, etc.). Discuss how the celebration is meant to bring good luck. Then

invite cooperative learning groups of five or six to plan a segment for a classroom Good Luck or New Year's celebration. Invite them to use some of the listed ideas and add others from their own or other ethnic groups in the surrounding area. Make materials available for costumes, masks, paper-lantern facsimiles, and other decorations. As groups ready their segments, work with the class to decide on a time and a sequence for the celebration. Suggest that one member of each cooperative learning group be ready to tell an audience which ethnic groups were the resources for the presentation. Students may wish to invite other classrooms or their families to come to the celebration.

Oral Language:

Old-Skill Interviews   Discuss why Pu Yee was able to teach Chin Chiang the dragon's dance. (She had learned and performed it when she was younger.) Invite students to interview an adult at home or in their neighborhood to find out about a skill or game the interviewee learned as a child and is willing to teach to the interviewer. Suggest that students practice the skill or game, then teach it to a small group of classmates.

 **Welcome to the Neighborhood!**

1. Complete the folder with pictures and facts about Chin Chiang's neighborhood, or about your own.
2. Cut out the folder and fold it along the lines.
3. Show your folder to some classmates. See if they can guess what neighborhood it tells about.

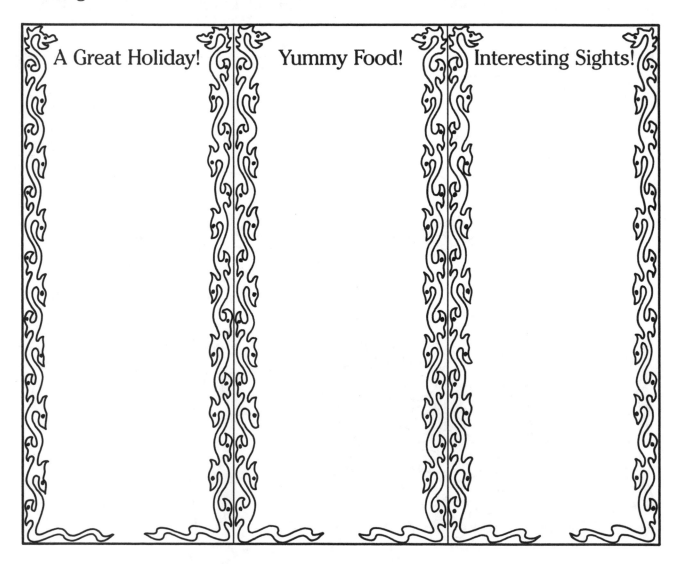

A Great Holiday!   Yummy Food!   Interesting Sights!

Fold
2

Fold
1

Name _____

Hooray for Chin Chiang!

1. Finish the prize badge to show why Chin Chiang wins it.
2. Color your badge and ribbon and cut them out. Attach the ribbon to the badge.
3. Put tape on the back so that you can wear your badge.

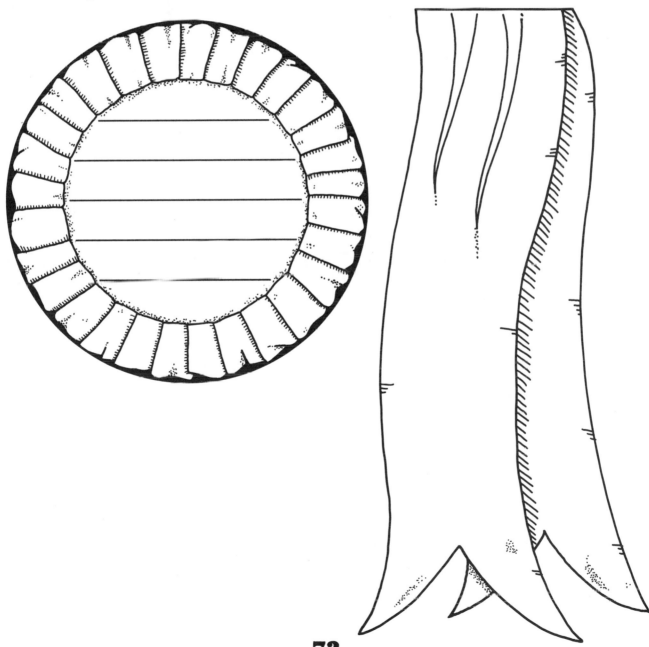

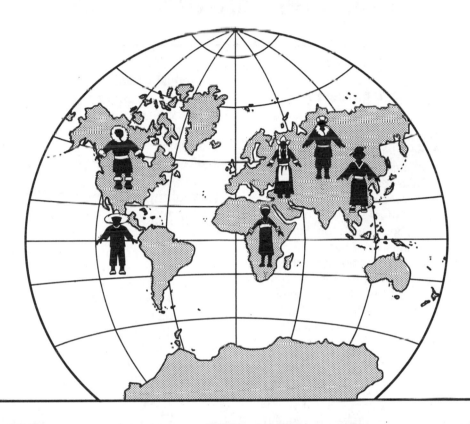

 **Chapter Book Level**

The Bear on the Moon

Joanne Ryder
Illustrated by Carol Lacey (Morrow 1991)

Summary:

Set in the Arctic and modeled on traditional origin tales, the story gives a fanciful version of how land emerged on earth, and describes the waxing and waning of the moon. The polar bear heroine, always swimming in an endless sea with other bears, becomes curious about the moon. Finally one night she climbs a stairway of light (the aurora borealis) to the sky, and touches down on the moon. She kicks large chunks of icy rock to earth, forming land, then returns to the Arctic. The polar bears and other creatures enjoy the solid land, but as the moon wanes and disappears, so does the land. The heroine joyfully watches the moon "grow" again, and when it is full climbs up to kick more solid land to earth. This, says the story, is what the bear continues to do to this very day when the moon is full, and explains why, if you use your imagination, you can see a bear on the moon.

Preparation:

Explain that the story is set in the Arctic. On a globe, point out the Arctic and Antarctic and invite students to tell what they know about the climate, land, water, and animals of those regions. Explain that though much of the story is make-believe, many of the words and pictures also tell about Arctic facts. Suggest that students listen and look to separate fact from fantasy.

As You Read

Invite students to tell why the bear thinks the moon is disappearing and then reappearing. Does the moon ever really go away? On the chalkboard or on poster paper, write students' ideas about the moon. Keep the list for reference in Extending Geography Skills.

To help students respond to the heroine's curiosity and steadfastness, invite them to tell about times when they were curious about something and could not get their questions answered by friends or family. What did the students do as a result: give up or search further? Did they succeed in their quest for an answer? How did this make them feel? How does the bear probably feel when she discovers the moon and finds a way to help her friends?

Extending Geography Skills:
Moon Phases

Invite pairs of students to take turns playing the roles of *Sun* and *Earth* in an activity which will help to explain the cycle of moon phases over the course of a month and why the polar bear in the story actually thought the moon periodically "went away."

You will need a bright flashlight, a sturdy chair, and a basketball or soccer ball. Explain to the class that (1.) the student holding the flashlight is the Sun; (2.) the student holding the ball is Earth;

(3) the ball itself is the moon. Ask "Earth" to move the moon by turning slowly around in a complete circle, as shown in the diagram, holding the

"moon" steady. Ask the student to describe the changing lighted shape, or "phase," on the moon as it moves. Explain to the class that the moon's trip around Earth actually lasts about thirty days. Invite volunteers to figure out how this time period is related to the cycle of months of the year. To verify responses and help students summarize the activity, display a monthly "moon" calendar. Invite students to observe the moon in the night sky two or three times during the month and check what they see with the moon phase shown on the calendar. Encourage students to invite family members to observe with them while the student explains why the moon has phases.

Making Connections

Science:
What's It Really Like?   Invite groups of four or five students to research and report on ideas and questions that came up as they read the story. Topics can emerge by brainstorming a list of questions with the class, for example: What are the "streamers of light" the bear sees in the sky? What kinds of animals and plants live in Arctic waters and on land? What is the climate of the Arctic like? Why is the Arctic sometimes called "the land of the midnight sun?" What are the differences and similarities between the Arctic and the Antarctic? Where are the North and South poles, and what do they represent? Suggest that groups assign roles so that they can share their findings with the class through maps, drawings, or models; or through a play in which a "polar bear" asks questions and other group members answer the questions.

Literature/Story Telling:
How It All Began   Review the first two pages of the story and discuss how the seals, owls, and polar bears tell about the beginnings of certain phenomena from their own points of view. Invite students to list phenomena that could be imaginatively explained in an origin story; examples are: sun, moon, stars, rainbows, the ocean, lightning, wind, the seasons, mountains, deserts. Then suggest that students make up an origin-story told from the point of view of a certain animal. For example: How might a cat explain the origin of the moon? How might an eagle explain the origin of lightning? How might a robin explain how the seasons of the year came to be? Invite students to share their stories in different ways. Some students may wish to write, illustrate, and read them aloud. Others might tell them aloud in a small story-circle. Partners or small groups might act their stories out or make taped "radio plays" of

them. You might set aside a morning or an afternoon in which all the stories can be shared in a Story-Cycle Marathon.

Art:
Ways of Seeing   Display a large color photo or color photocopy of the moon in the center of the board. Explain that while the "shadows" are actually the moon's valleys and mountains, it's possible to see in them many different figures and shapes. Point out the "bear on the moon" shown in the last book illustration and invite students to tell about other figures they have seen, such as "the man in the moon" and "the lady in the chair." Invite students to find other figures in the moon photo, or in the real moon, and make labelled paintings or drawings of them. Place the students' work around the bulletin board photo. Students can share their work by pointing out the moon "shadows" on which their drawings are based. Invite interested students to write a story to accompany their picture. Place the stories in a folder near the bulletin board for students to read and discuss independently.

What Comes Next?

1. In the frame after each pair of pictures, draw something that will probably happen next.
2. Cut your pictures out along the dotted lines.
3. Scramble your pictures. Then use them to play a What-Comes-Next game with a classmate.

Bear Tales

1. In each section of the moon, write something you liked about the bear.
2. Color the moon. Paste the picture on cardboard and cut it out.
3. Make a hole at the top and pull yarn through.
4. Hang the moon in a place where your classmates can enjoy it.

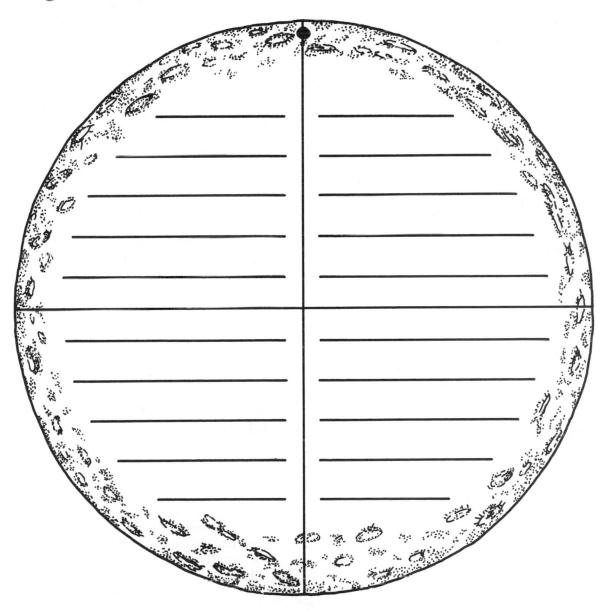

Washington Irving's
Rip Van Winkle

adapted by Thomas Locker (Dial 1988)

Summary:

Rip lives in a Dutch settlement in New York's Hudson Valley in the mid-18th century. He is a good-natured but lazy fellow, hardly able to support his family. One day, to escape his wife's complaints, he goes hunting in the hills. There he meets a group of Dutchmen dressed in the clothes of the century before. They are playing ninepins (bowling) and drinking from a keg. Rip takes a drink, too, and falls into a deep sleep. His nap lasts 20 years, so that when he wakes up he finds that he and his hometown have changed a great deal. He is finally recognized by his grown daughter, and his neighbors believe his story: legend has it that the ghosts of Henry Hudson and his crew come back to the mountains from time to time to play ninepins in the hollows. When the thunder rolls, say the local people, this is the sound of Hudson and his men at their game again.

Preparation:

On a map of the United States, point to the New York seacoast and the Hudson River. Explain that about 350 years ago Dutch settlers came to this region and built towns along the river. Preview the landscape illustrations and discuss what the land looked like then. Invite students to tell how the land has probably changed since then, and what remains the same. Explain that the story is about a man who had a hard time with changes.

As You Read

As students discuss the picture of the Dutchmen playing ninepins, take time out to show and discuss an enlarged copy of the map below. Explain that Henry Hudson was an Englishman who made four voyages to America during the years 1607 and 1611. Invite students to point out the three geographic features named after him (Hudson Bay, Hudson Strait, and the Hudson River). Explain that on the 1610 voyage, Hudson was working for a company in Holland, and the crew of his ship the

Half Moon was made up of Dutch sailors. To help students get an idea of the small size of ships in those days, invite them to count the men shown in the picture (13) and then add seven. This (20) was the size of Hudson's crew.

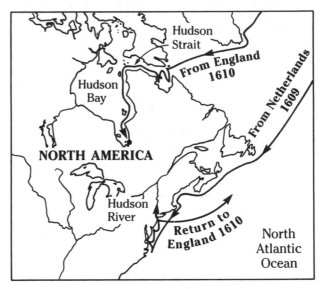

Invite students to read the pictures to find some of the changes that Rip encountered in his home and village when he returned 20 years later. What was the "strange red, white, and blue flag"? What important thing had happened during Rip's long sleep? (The United States had been formed.) What do students think might have been most confusing to Rip?

Extending Geography Skills:
Analyzing Place-Names

1. **Names on the Land**   Display a political map of the United States. Explain that the names of land forms, bodies of water, states, and cities in a region give clues to who the first inhabitants were and the lands from which explorers and settlers came. Read some of the many Native American place names that range from coast to coast and invite students to tell why Native American place names predominate all over the nation. Remind students that *Rip Van Winkle* is

a Dutch person's name, and that there are many Dutch place names in New York, such as *Catskills, Spuyten Divil, Harlem,* and *Poughkeepsie*. List clusters of place-names in Spanish, French, and German and invite small groups of students to find the clusters on the map and tell classmates what this indicates about the European origins of the first settlers.

2. **If Rip Had Lived Here**   Display a large map of your state. Invite cooperative learning groups of four or five to retell the story, setting it in their area and using local place names. To establish who the "ghosts" will be, one or two members can research to find out who the first European explorers of the region were. After the group establishes the story sequence, two or three members can prepare illustrations and a map to accompany the story which traces their hero's or heroine's adventure. The student presenting the final story to the class can indicate the route on the display-map. Put the finished stories in a folder near the map for students to read and discuss independently.

Literature/Art:
Local Lore   Plan a trip to the library, local museum, or historical society to listen to a staffer tell about legends of your area. If the legend emanates from a place in or near your community, you might organize a field trip to visit the site. Back in the classroom, invite students to draw or paint pictures depicting the place and the legend that goes with it. Suggest that students write sentence-captions for their art. Display the finished work around the classroom.

Drama:
Rip on the Radio   Invite small groups of students to make a taped radio-play reenacting *Rip Van Winkle*. Suggest that students create sound effects for such things as Rip's dog barking, the sound of bowling balls, rolls of thunder, and the crash of a waterfall. Put the finished tapes in a Listening Center for students to listen to as they review the illustrations.

Oral Language:
Time-Capsule Tales   Invite groups of nine or ten students to sit in a circle and close their eyes as you take them on an imaginary journey into the future. As you tell the story, emphasize—without giving specific details—the kinds of things that are changing as the students take their "20-year-nap": buildings, ways of making a living, forms of transportation, clothing, ways of communicating, games, music, and so forth. Then ask students to "wake up from their nap" and tell others in the group what they saw in their mind's eye as you told the story. Invite interested students to draw a picture or write a story about the world-of-the-future the group envisioned.

Name _____

Log It In!

As they explored, ship captains kept logs, or records to tell what they saw and did. Imagine that you are a captain. Fill in the log to tell about a day of exploration. Share and compare your log with ones that your classmates make.

CAPTAIN'S LOG

Aboard the ship _____

Date: _____

Today we are sailing _____

The weather is _____

We are searching for _____

The crew was glad when _____

_____

_____

Several sailors became afraid when _____

_____

_____

By tomorrow, I hope _____

_____

Captain _____

(Signature)

Name _____

Speak, Wolf!

Follow Rip's dog, Wolf, along the path. At each stop read what Rip does. Write what Wolf might say if he could speak.

3. Rip leans back on a tree and drinks from the keg

Wolf Says:
_____
_____
_____

2. Rip sees the little men bowling

Wolf Says:
_____
_____

4. Rip falls fast asleep

Wolf Says:
_____
_____
_____

1. Wolf follows Rip into the mountains

Wolf Says:
_____
_____

Start here

83

Death of the Iron Horse

Paul Goble (Bradbury Press 1987)

Summary:

The Cheyenne still tell the story of the time (on August 6, 1867) when a group of their young men rode bravely out to fight off "the iron horse," the freight train that was traveling along tracks newly laid for the transcontinental railway system. In building this system, the white entrepreneurs had displaced or killed thousands of Native Americans and had killed most of the buffalo and ruined much of the land on which they grazed. The young men, determined to save their families from more disaster, pull up a section of track, derail the iron horse, and triumphantly carry away many of the goods in it. Though their triumph is short-lived (the railroad-building and the removal of Native Americans from their ancestral lands continued), the story is honored today in memory of the brave people who tried to defend their families' way of life.

Preparation:

On a political map of the United States, point out the setting of the story: the area in Nebraska between Omaha and North Platte. Invite students to study the illustrations on the title and copyright/introductory pages to predict which two different groups of people will be involved in the story and which two different uses to which this land was put in the mid-19th century. Read the story introduction.

As You Read

Explain that by 1860 white settlers had built communities from coast to coast, and that the United States government was backing a plan to build a railroad to link the coasts. On a topographical map, point out Sacramento, California, and Omaha, Nebraska, and explain that one group would lay tracks eastward and the other westward (roughly following the 42nd parallel) until the tracks met. Explain that all along this route were the communities and vast ancestral

hunting grounds of thousands of Native Americans. Invite students to fill in a chalkboard chart idea web like the one below to suggest how the ideas about land use conflicted.

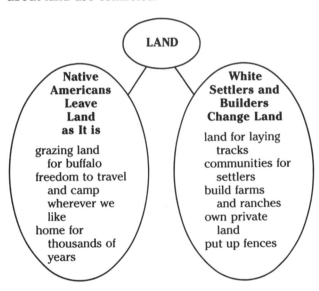

To help students respond to the derailing and ransacking of the train, you might compare the threat the "iron horse" presented to the threat of a "flying saucer" attack today. In the latter case, why wouldn't we know what the saucers were made of or how they moved? How might you respond if you knew that in other places where they landed the flying saucers had brought death and destruction to your people? You can use the actions of the young men in the story to initiate an open-ended discussion about their motives and the pros and cons of their behavior.

Extending Geography Skills: Mapping Disputed Areas

To help students understand that conflicts about land-use are on-going, place a map of your community or state at the center of the board under the heading *How Shall We Use the Earth?* and invite student-partners to help you complete the display. Partners can first listen and look via television and newspapers for news of disputes about how land and adjoining water in your community or state is to be used. Examples are: preserve wetlands for wildlife, or build houses? Use available land for dumps and landfill, or build parks there? keep old historic houses intact, or tear them down to build needed low-cost housing; drill for oil offshore, or maintain the ocean as it is? Cut down forests to provide jobs for lumberjacks, or preserve forests to keep endangered species extant? After partners have decided on an issue, they can make *Pro* and *Con* lists to clarify the different points of view. Ask partners to circle the disputed areas on the map. Post the lists around the map, and attach them with yarn to the circled areas. Invite partners to present their lists orally to the class. Encourage the class to discuss and debate the issues. Suggest that students find ways to make their opinions known outside the classroom, for example, through letter-writing campaigns or a poster display in a corridor or library.

Making Connections:

Literature:
Class Historians   Review with students why the Cheyenne still tell the story of the Iron Horse and honor the young men involved in stopping it. Invite students to tell about family members, friends, or neighbors who work hard for causes they believe in. Write suggestions on the chalkboard and discuss why these people are honored in their communities. Invite students to write and illustrate true stories about some of these people. After students read and show their stories to classmates, put the stories in a *Local Heroes* folder and suggest that students read and discuss them with a partner.

Art:
Story Mural   Invite cooperative learning groups of four or five to plan and make a section for a time-line mural that retells *Death of the Iron Horse*. First, ask the class to brainstorm a sequential chalkboard list of the main events in the story. Suggest that each group choose one of the events to portray. After the group has decided what details their mural-section will show, each group member can be responsible for painting specific details. The group can appoint a student to tell the class what their finished mural-section shows. Each section can be presented in the story sequence, then mounted in the display area before the next section is presented, until the whole mural is in place. Invite small groups of students to use the mural as they retell the story orally together.

Thinking Skills:
Picture Viewpoints   With a small group of students, discuss the final picture in the book, first to identify the modern inventions it shows (windmill, jet planes, train, silos, water tower, power lines), and then to find a picture clue showing the author/artist's opinion about what people have done to the land in recent times (the rubble and litter along the tracks). Which way of life—the old way or the new way—does the author probably respect more? Invite students to discuss in what ways they agree or disagree with him. Suggest that students draw pictures to show how the best of the old and the best of the new might be combined. Students can show and explain their pictures to the class and answer questions from the audience.

Plan a Place

The space below stands for an empty block in your community. What do you think the block should be used for? Choose not more than five of the things shown in the pictures. Cut out the pictures and paste them on the block. Show your block map to a friend. Tell why you chose each thing, and why you left the others out.

Name _____

The History of You

Imagine that it is twenty years from now. Someone is writing about you in a history book. What do you want the story to say? Fill in the blanks to finish the story. Share your story with a friend, then ask your friend to draw a picture to go with it.

The Story of _____

_____ was born in _____
(your name)   (place)

on _____ _____, 19 _____. As a child, _____
   (month)   (day)   (year)   (your name)

wanted to be a _____. _____ dreamed about
                    (job or career)   (She, He)

_____.
              (a great deed you want to do)

_____ wanted to do this so that people
          (your name)

would _____
              (something good you want to happen)

_____.

_____ is an important person because
          (your name)

_____
              (why you will be important)

_____.

Family Pictures

Carmen Lomas Garza
(Children's Book Press 1990)

Summary:

Through words and pictures, the author, a major Mexican-American artist, describes her childhood in Kingsville, Texas, just over the border from Mexico. The richly-detailed illustrations show traditional games and festivals, special family outings, and everyday activities involved with gathering and preparing food and visiting relatives. The text is in English and Spanish.

Preparation:

1. Display a political map of North America as you explain that the story tells about a Mexican family that moved to Kingsville, Texas, about 100 miles from the Mexican border.
2. If possible, have a Spanish-speaking student, teacher, or community-resource person tape-record all or some of the Spanish renditions of the text. Make copies of the Spanish text for interested students to follow along with as they listen to the tapes.

As You Read

Invite students to tell why the climate, land, and vegetation shown in the picture of the fair in Reynosa, Mexico (page 5) look just like these same geographical characteristics as they are shown in pictures of life in Kingsville, Texas. To facilitate responses, next to the political map you displayed for *Preparation,* above, display a topographical map or global view of the same region.

To help students respond to the author/artist's special memories, invite them to fill a chalkboard idea web with details under the general categories she tells about. Invite students to tell about experiences of their own that fall into these categories.

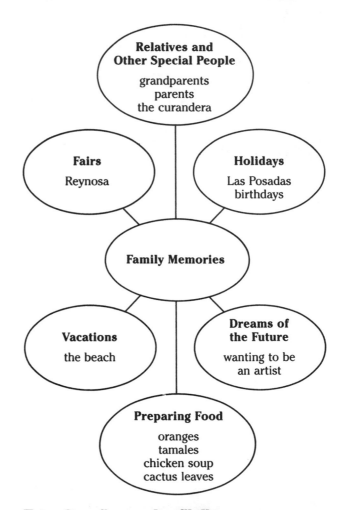

Relatives and Other Special People
grandparents
parents
the curandera

Fairs
Reynosa

Holidays
Las Posadas
birthdays

Family Memories

Vacations
the beach

Dreams of the Future
wanting to be an artist

Preparing Food
oranges
tamales
chicken soup
cactus leaves

Extending Geography Skills: Investigating Changing Boundaries

1. **History in Maps**   To help students understand that the boundaries on a political map show who owns or governs the land at a particular time in history, make and distribute copies of an outline map of the 48 contiguous United States today and of the map below, which shows Mexican and United States boundaries about 1790.

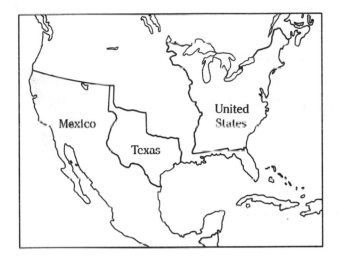

Invite students to compare the maps to determine where the Spanish language and Spanish customs predominated 200 years ago. Review some of the traditions described in *Family Pictures*. Invite students to overlay their maps to determine which parts of Mexico eventually became part of the United States, through wars or treaties. Discuss which of the following seem to last longer: languages and customs, or political boundaries? political boundaries or landforms and climate?

2. **Dividing Up the Land**   Making "crumple maps" is a hands-on activity that helps cement the concept of the difference between land forms and political divisions of land. Distribute small sheets of drawing paper, explaining that the paper stands for "land." Ask students to crumple up the paper, then open it. Next, students can trace each crumple line with a black marker to make "boundaries" on the land. Invite students to make up and write names for the countries outlined on their crumple maps. As students share their maps with the class, it will become obvious to them that the boundaries are different, even though the basic shape of the land is the same.

Making Connections

Literature/Oral Language

Explain how *Family Pictures* came to be: the artist, Carmen Lomas Garza, first painted the pictures about her childhood, then talked with a friend about them. The friend set the artist's words down in writing. Suggest that student partners follow this procedure as each partner paints and describes his or her own family picture. If possible, make tape recorders available so that the writing-partner can check to make sure he or she has covered all the important details the speaking-partner described.

Students can refer to the idea web above to get ideas for their pictures. Display the pictures and stories under the bulletin board head *Our Family Pictures.*

Social Studies:
Community Interviews   Invite volunteers to recall interesting stories older relatives or friends have told about their own childhoods. Explain that these stories (often beginning "When I was a child . . .") about the past are *history,* full of important ideas and facts about bygone times. If the stories are not written down, however, they eventually are forgotten and "lost." Suggest that students conduct interviews at home to collect and write "When I Was a Child . . ." stories. Ask interviewers to concentrate on questions about the *place* in which the interviewee grew up. After students share their written stories with the class, ask two or three volunteers to organize them for a reading table in folders according to the geographic locations of the stories, for example *Stories About Growing Up in a Big City* or *Stories About Growing Up in Mexico.*

Game:
Geography-walk   Invite cooperative learning groups of four or five to adapt the Cakewalk game described in *Family Pictures* to make it a geography game for the playground or gym. You might give an example: each square can name a place the class has recently studied or visited; when the music stops, the person in the center selects and calls out a place-name from a box; if the player standing on that place-name can tell a fact about the place, he or she wins a "Geography Ribbon" (prepared by the group in advance). To generate ideas for the groups, suggest that the class first brainstorm a chalkboard list of other categories of geography words that the squares might contain, such as weather words, landform and water body words, ecology words, and names of plants and animals of different regions. After the group has decided together on the basic format of their game, the following roles can be assigned: marking off the playing area with chalk or tape; writing the words in the squares; writing the same words for the slips in the box; explaining the game to players; turning the tape-recorded music on and off; deciding whether the player's response is correct.

Drive and Find

1. Cut out the car. Put it on Kingsville, Texas.
2. Use it on the roads to find the places in the questions.

3. Drive to a ranch. What's its name?

_____

4. Drive to a National Seashore. What's its name? _____

_____

5. Drive to a Bay. What's its name? _____

_____

6. Drive to a Gulf. What's its name? _____

7. Drive to another country. What's its name?

_____

8. Park at Reynosa and go to the fair!

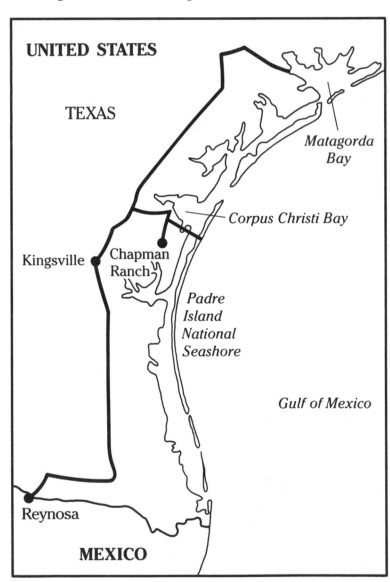

UNITED STATES

TEXAS

Matagorda Bay

Corpus Christi Bay

Kingsville • Chapman Ranch

Padre Island National Seashore

Gulf of Mexico

Reynosa •

MEXICO

 **Tell Us About It!**

1. Draw a picture to go with each title below.
2. In the balloon, write what you think or feel about each place.
3. Cut out the pages.
4. Make a cover for your Family Pictures book. Show and read your book with a classmate.

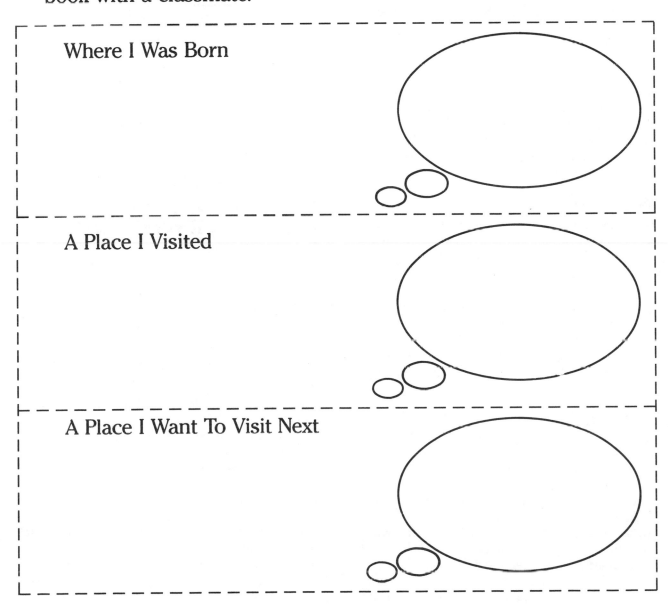

Where I Was Born

A Place I Visited

A Place I Want To Visit Next

Sarah, Plain & Tall

Patricia MacLachlan (Harper & Row 1985)

Summary:

In response to an advertisement common about a hundred years ago, Sarah Wheaton travels from Maine to a mid-western farm to see whether she wants to settle down with the widower Jacob and his children, Anna and Caleb. The children and their father love Sarah's feistiness, warmth, and imagination, but fear she misses the sea so much that she will leave them to return to her home. When Sarah goes to town in the wagon, Caleb especially fears that she will never come back. But Sarah does, bearing with her a parcel of colored pencils that link the colors of her sea with the colors of the children's prairie home, and signalling that she has made her decision to stay and become part of the family.

Preparation:

On a topographical map, point out Maine, then the American prairie states. Invite students to use the map to tell about differences in land and water. Explain that the story tells about a woman who moved from Maine to the prairie more than a hundred years ago, when railroads were new, airplanes did not exist, and every move was thus a "big" move and likely to be permanent. Ask students to predict what a person from Maine might miss if she or he moved hundreds of miles inland.

As You Read

Encourage students to discuss what Sarah misses from her old home in Maine (such as swimming in the sea, ocean colors, watching seals, sliding down sand dunes, her brother's fishing boat) and how Jacob, Anna, and Caleb try to replicate some of these experiences for her on their midwest farm. Invite students to name some of the most obvious differences, such as salt water/fresh water; sand/grass; prairie flowers/seaside flowers.

While Maine and the prairie are quite different, Sarah and Caleb are much alike. To help students compare these two characters, invite them to fill in a chalkboard character chart like the one below as they read the story. Discuss how their likenesses pull Sarah and Caleb together.

Character	How Does the Character Feel "Different"?	What Does the Character Miss?	What Does the Character Learn?
Caleb	thinks he is loud and pesky	his mother's songs	that Sarah loves him
Sarah	tall, plain, unneeded in her brother's home	the sea her home in Maine	how to enjoy a prairie home that Jacob and the children love and need her

Extending Geography Skills: Comparing Map Keys and Legends

In a central location, provide a variety of United States maps, such as topographical maps, highway maps, political maps, views from space, historical maps, and goods-and-resources maps. Review with students how Sarah associated certain colors—gray, green, and blue—with her home in Maine. Invite student partners to choose one of the maps and discover how it uses colors to indicate special facts about places. Partners might start by reading the title of their map to find out its purpose, next study the legend to find out what particular colors or symbols stand for, and then locate the Maine seacoast and trace Sarah's approximate route from there to the central part of the country. Suggest that partners note differences, as indicated by the colors and symbols, as they move from one region to another. Then invite partners to show their maps to the class and tell about major differences in regions and how the colors on their maps signal them. The class will soon note that the same color may be used in different ways on different maps, depending on what aspect of a region the map is intended to show.

Making Connections

Art:

Pictures Praising Places   At the center of the bulletin board, place a picture of Sarah. At the top, under the book title, make heads for two columns on either side of the figure: *The Best Things About the Farm* and *The Best Things About the Sea.* Invite students to brainstorm a chalkboard list of things or activities Sarah might put in each column. Suggest that each student choose one item from each list and make construction-paper cut-out pictures of the items. As students affix their pictures in the bulletin-board columns, invite them to tell why Sarah likes each thing. Suggest that students use the finished bulletin board as a reference as they retell the story to a partner or small group.

Language:

Delightful Dialects   Call on a volunteer to retell the incident in which Sarah teaches the children a "Maine word" for "yes" (*ayuh*). Discuss how people in different parts of the country, or even in different towns or neighborhoods in the same general area, may use different words to indicate the same thing. Some examples are flapjacks, griddle cakes, pancakes; grinder, sub, hero; skillet, frying pan, spider; snapbeans, green beans, stringbeans. Invite students who have moved to your community from other areas or who visit relatives in other places to tell about some of the different words and expressions they encounter. List students' contributions on the chalkboard. Suggest that interested students use the board list to begin an *All-American Dictionary,* adding to it as they come across other regional expressions in books or outside the classroom. Keep the Dictionary on a reading table for students to refer to as they write stories set in different places.

Creative Writing:

Shape Letters   Invite students to recall the many different animals mentioned in the story, for example, Sarah's cat Seal, the dogs Lottie and Nick, the horses Old Bess and Jack, the three lambs, the chickens, and the seal that Sarah remembers petting back home in Maine. Invite cooperative learning groups of four to choose one of the animals, imagine that it can write, and work together to write a "shape letter" from the animal to another one, describing some part of the story from the animal-writer's point of view. After the group has decided on the basic message, roles can be assigned: two students to design and cut a pattern of the animal's shape, to use for the covers and pages of the letter; one student to write the letter; one student to draw a picture on one of the shape-pages. After the groups have shared their letters with the class, put all the letters in a cardboard *Sarah's Mailbox.* Suggest that students read the letters to a partner.

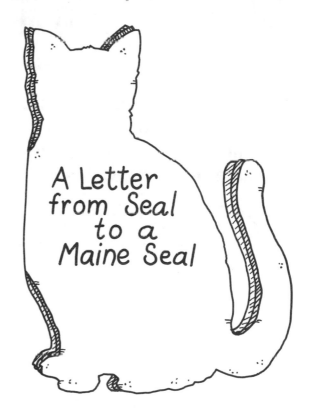

93

A Quilt for Sarah

Design a quilt for Sarah. In four squares, show some things to remind her of Maine. In the other four squares, draw things that make her happy about the farm she lives on now. Show your quilt design to a classmate. Tell why each square is important to Sarah.

Let's Face It!

1. On the left side, draw a face to show how the person feels at the beginning of the story.
2. On the right side, draw a face to show how the person feels at the end of the story.
3. Cut out the puppets.
4. Fold the right side over so that the puppet has two sides. Paste the sides together.
5. Use your puppets to act out a conversation between Sarah and Caleb.

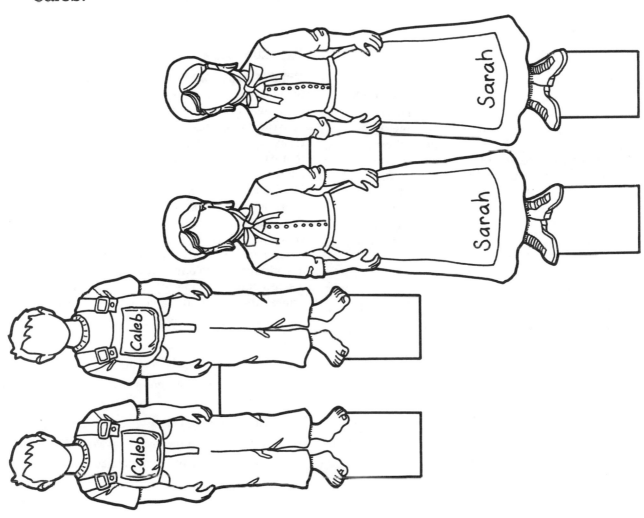

Ashanti to Zulu

Margaret Musgrove
Illustrated by Leo and Diane Dillon (Dial 1976)

Summary:

Using an alphabet-book approach, the author and artists briefly describe a custom of each of 26 African groups, just a few of the hundreds of different peoples and language groups of Saharan and sub-Saharan Africa. Because of the great topographical and climatic differences across the African continent, each group had developed distinctly different ways of meeting basic needs and of celebrating important occasions.

Preparation:

1. Make copies of the map on the last page of the book and distribute them to students.
2. On a world map, point out and name the seven continents: Asia, Africa, North America, South America, Antarctica, Europe, and Australia. Explain that the book tells about some of the groups of people who live on one of these continents. Invite volunteers to study the shapes of the continents on the world map and refer to the map you have distributed to figure out what continent they will read about.
3. If possible, then display a large topographical/political map of Africa for students to refer to as they read the book.

As You Read

Suggest that students find and circle the name of each group on their map-copies as they read or listen to the page. As a collating activity, invite volunteers to point out on the large world map or map of Africa the approximate location of this group. Discuss how the name of the nation or region on the political map is not the same as the name of the people. To clarify the idea that people of many different groups may live within a single nation, use the United States as an example, inviting students to name some of the different ethnic groups they know of who live within the United States and are thus Americans.

Invite students to help you fill in a chalkboard chart like the one below that checks off parallels in their own lives to each of the important events or activities discussed in the book. Reserve or copy the completed chart for use in the second cooperative learning activity.

In Africa	Here	
	Yes	No
Ashanti: Clothes for special occasions	✔	
Baule: Legends and stories about history	✔	
Chagga: Children forming groups	✔	

Extending Geography Skills: Determining Elements of Continents

Invite students to work in seven cooperative learning groups to find out about what a continent is. Write the names of the continents on the chalkboard (see *Preparation,* above) and suggest that each group choose one to investigate. (Some authorities consider Europe not a continent in itself, but a peninsula of Asia, with the whole land mass being called Eurasia. If you wish to follow this school of thought, suggest that the groups choosing Europe and Asia merge into a single group.) Each group should have access to either a world map or to a map of their continent. Also discuss and distribute to each group a list of "clues" that will guide them in their investigation:

Name of Continent _____
1. Is it a very large mass of land? _____
2. Does it have large flat areas? _____
3. Does it have a least one large mountain range? ___
   What is one range's name? _____
4. Is it surrounded or nearly surrounded by water? ___
   What is the name of one of the water bodies?
   _____

Group members can assign the roles of finding the data on the map, recording it on the clue list, and sharing the list with the class while pointing out relevant features on the map. Conclude the activity by inviting the class as a whole to develop a definition of *continent,* using the words in the clue list for ideas. Ask a volunteer to check the class's definition with one in a dictionary. Suggest that two or three students make a folder for the groups' completed clue lists. Put the folder on a table in your social studies center and suggest that students use it to make up Continent Quiz Games to play with a partner.

Making Connections

Literature/Language:

Alphabetical Explorations   Invite cooperative learning groups of five or six to write and illustrate their own books about traditions and ways of life, using the alphabet as an organizational method. Suggest that the class first work together to brainstorm a list of geographic areas, from large to small, that might be covered in the books, for example, a home, a neighborhood, a community, a town or city, a state, a region of the United States, or the United States as a whole. Each group can then choose one of the areas to concentrate on. Explain that while groups need not cover all 26 letters in their books, they should try to list as many customs, games, holidays, ceremonies, special foods, organizations, and so forth, as possible, then arrange the pages and picture

alphabetically. One member's role might be to list the group's ideas, then help make drawing, writing, and cover-and-binding assignments. Suggest that the group share its book with the class by having each member show and read the pages he or she has made. Put the completed books on a reading table for students to read and discuss with a partner.

Visual Literacy/Art;

Picture This   Explain to the class that the illustrators of *Ashanti to Zulu* included the following in almost every picture: a man, a woman, a child, a house, an artifact, and a local animal. Invite students to review the pictures to find these elements. Discuss the likenesses and differences they observe among the groups. You might also point out the knot that occurs in the corners of the frame for each picture; this design is based on the Kano Knot, and stands for "endless searching." Discuss why this is a good symbol for people who like to explore the world. Suggest that students make paintings or drawings of their own neighborhood that include the same elements as the book pictures, and make up their own symbols to use in a drawn frame. Students can share their work by asking classmates to find and identify the elements and guess what the symbols mean. Display the pictures around the room, or put them in a folder on a reading table for students to refer to for story ideas.

Name _____

Shapes of the World

The shapes below are the shapes of the seven continents.

1. Color the shapes to make them look like land. Cut the shapes out and paste them on blue paper.
2. Find the name of each continent by matching the shape to one on a map or globe. Write the name on the back of the continent-cut out.
3. Use your continent flash-cards in a game with a classmate.

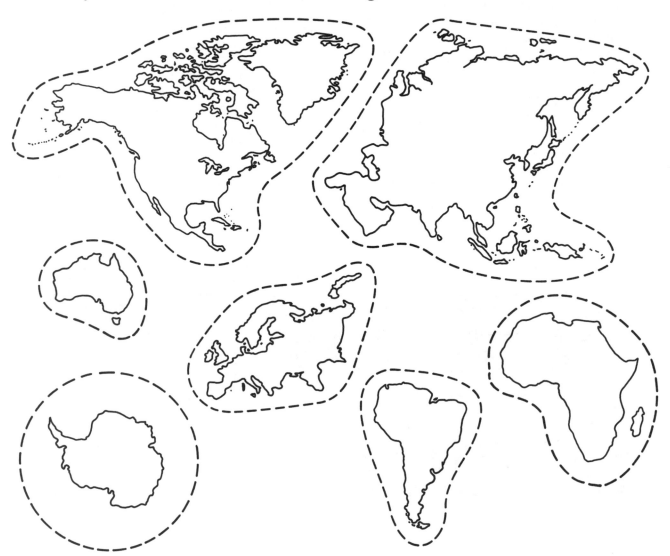

 # Your Worlds

1. Starting with the ring labelled Planet, complete each label to tell more about where you live.
2. Color each ring a different color.
3. Cut the circle out along the dotted line. Put a hole near the top, then a string through the hole. Color the back of the circle.
4. Display your world where your classmates can enjoy it.

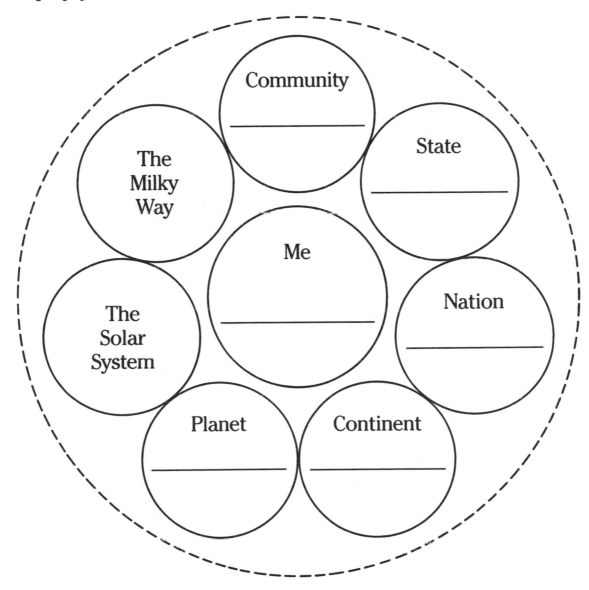

Stone Fox

John Reynolds Gardiner
Illustrated by Marcia Sewall (HarperCollins 1980)

Summary:

Little Willy lives with his Grandfather on a potato farm near Jackson, Wyoming. When Grandfather falls into a deep depression over his inability to pay the land taxes, Willy decides to help out by entering his dog Searchlight in the National Dogsled Race, where the first prize is $500. Willy's major opponent is the Native American, Stone Fox, who races his team of Malamutes each year and inevitably wins, using the prize money to buy back land he feels the white settlers have stolen from his people. The plucky Searchlight, neck and neck with Stone Fox's team, dies of exhaustion just before he reaches the finish line. Stone Fox stops his own team and the others as well so that Willy can carry the body of his gallant dog across the finish line and win.

Preparation:

Point out the city of Jackson, Wyoming, and the Teton Mountains on a topographical map. Invite students to indicate on the map the mountain range of which the Tetons are a part (the Rocky Mountains) and to discuss what they know about the mountain terrain and climate. Show the book cover and preview some of the illustrations so that students can check and verify their ideas.

As You Read

Discuss the many decisions Willy has to make and invite students to tell why he chose certain actions and rejected others. For example, why did Willy choose to take care of his Grandfather himself rather than let Mrs. Peacock care for him? Why did Willy decide to work to keep the farm instead of selling it? How did Willy decide to harvest the potatoes when he could not rent horses to pull the plow? Invite students to tell how Willy and his grandfather feel about the land and how each of Willy's decisions is based on his ultimate goal: to

keep the land so that his grandfather will take heart and get well.

At the conclusion, students can respond via a Discussion Web to the problems raised when Willy wins the race at the expense of Searchlight's life. Copy the Discussion Web below on the chalkboard and invite students to discuss the issues and fill out the web. Invite students to work as partners.

Discussion: "The Race" in *Stone Fox*
Reasons

Did Willy deserve to win the race?

NO   YES

Extending Geography Skills: Mapping the Mountains

Six cooperative learning groups can first research the six chief ranges of the Rockies, then contribute their findings to a bulletin board which describes the ranges in pictures and captions.

1. Introduce the activity by explaining that the Rockies are the largest mountain system in North America. The chain is more than 3000 miles long, and about 350 miles wide in some places. (You may wish to point out that in the United States the Rockies form the Continental Divide: rivers flow from the western slopes to the Pacific Ocean, and from the eastern slopes to the Atlantic.) Write the following list on the chalkboard and invite volunteers to identify the ranges on a topographical map as you read the list:
   1. Southern Rockies: from the Sangre de Cristo range in New Mexico to central Colorado.
   2. Middle Rockies: from northwestern Colorado and northern Utah to the upper Yellowstone River in Montana.

3. **Northern Rockies:** from southern Idaho to the border between the U.S. and Canada.

4. **Canadian Rockies:** from the Canadian border north through British Columbia and Alberta.

5. **Selwyn Mountains:** northward beyond the Liard River in northern Canada

6. **Brooks Range:** across northern Alaska to north of the Arctic Circle.

2. Suggest that each cooperative learning group choose one of the six ranges for its project. Group assignments can include the following: (1.) using topographical maps to find the highest peaks in the chain; (2.) using political maps to find major cities in the chain; (3.) researching to find national parks and sites of historical interest in the chain; (4.) drawing pictures to illustrate the data from 1, 2, and 3; (5.) writing brief captions to go with the pictures.

3. Groups can share their work with the class by contributing it to a *Rocky Mountains* bulletin board. Under that head, display a construction paper silhouette of the Rockies from north to south. Working through the six ranges from south to north, groups can appoint spokespersons to attach the pictures and labels to either side of the silhouette, telling the class about each feature as they do so.

Invite students to use the display: to find settings for telling their own stories modeled on *Stone Fox*; for writing travel brochures; for planning "dream" vacations; for investigating further to find out about and report to the class about wildlife in each chain; for making up arithmetic word problems based on the comparative heights of mountains in the Rockies; to add information to the display that tells how the Rockies were formed geologically.

Making Connections

Literature/Writing:

What If . . . Stories   Invite students to write paragraphs telling what might have happened if various events had taken a different turn, or if characters had made other choices. Introduce the activity by writing some examples on the chalkboard, then invite students to make up "what if's . . ." of their own. Add their suggestions to the board list. Examples are: What if the banker had not let Willy withdraw his saving from the bank? What if Stone Fox had not let Willy win? What if Searchlight had not died? What if Grandfather decided to sell the farm? Suggest that students choose one of these "if's" or another one to develop in their paragraphs and to illustrate with a drawing. After students have shared their work with the class, put the paragraphs and pictures in a folder on a reading table for students to read and discuss with a partner.

Math:

Book Quiz   Invite interested students to make up word problems loosely based on the story materials, for example: the number of potatoes Willy and Searchlight can plow in certain periods of time; the amount of money Willy and Grandfather can save or earn; the distance a Malamute and Searchlight can pull a sled in a certain number of minutes. You might also give students access to a road map of Wyoming and adjoining states and invite them to make up problems that involve using the distance scale on the map or the labels that indicate the altitudes of landforms. Ask students to present their word problems to the class, and encourage the problem-solvers to explain how they arrived at their answers. Then put the word problems in a folder in the math center for students to solve on their own.

Exploring With Stone Fox

Imagine that you are a wilderness guide. You are guiding travelers through the Rockies. In the balloons, write how you'd finish each sentence. Show and read your finished picture-strip to a classmate.

I love these mountains because
_____
_____

The Rockies are important because
_____
_____

My sled dogs like the weather here because
_____
_____

If you visit me here, I will introduce you to
_____
_____

Actions and Feelings

1. Complete the chart by writing about an event in the story that gave you the feeling listed at the left.
2. Cut along the dotted lines.
3. Play a game with a partner. Use your and your partner's strips to see which of your ideas match. Discuss the ideas that don't match.

Feeling	Event
Worried	
Sad	
Excited	
Angry	
Happy	

The Moon of the Alligators

Jean Craighead George
Illustrated by Michael Rothman
(HarperCollins 1991)

Summary:

In the Florida Everglades, the alligator is the "farmer," keeping the water clean of algae so that other creatures can live there, in turn attracting and sustaining a rich variety of birds and mammals. As the dry season sets in in October, the alligator grows increasingly desperate for food. The story tracks her journey during this month, and also describes the first years of her life. The intricate inter-relationships of plants and animals in the Everglades are threatened by canals, farming, and building projects. The detailed and lyrical descriptions of life cycles and seasons in this huge river show what would be lost if the Everglades ceased to be.

Preparation:

1. On a topographical map of the American Southeast, point out the area covered by the Everglades: from Lake Okechobee south to Florida Bay. Invite students to share questions they may have about this area. List questions on the chalkboard and ask students to look and listen for answers as they read.
2. Read the author's introduction to the book, in which she explains why she calls her series *The Thirteen Moons*. Suggest that students listen to the story to find out why she calls October "the moon of the Alligator" and why she says that the alligator has its own "inner clock."

As You Read

Invite students to help you develop a chalkboard timeline like the one below to trace the cycle of wet and dry seasons in the Everglades. Use the timeline as a reference-point for reviewing important events in the cycle before going on to the next sections of the story.

October	November– May	June– September
Alligator is very hungry. Dry season begins. River water lowers.	Drought. Animals come to alligator pool to live. Alligator has food.	Wet season. River grows. Alligator's food can swim away.

Take time out to discuss phrases and sentences that the students find particularly vivid and that help them form mental pictures of the events or animals being described. Invite volunteers to organize a *Describing Nature* notebook listing some of the phrases. (This should be an optional activity.) Encourage students to refer to the notebook as they discuss and review the *The Moon of the Alligators*. Students can also add to the notebook as they come across phrases in other books that vividly describe places and life forms, using the notebook as a reference when they do their own descriptive writing.

Extending Geography Skills: Understanding Chains of Life

Invite students to help you make a bulletin board display showing the ways plants and animals of the Everglades sustain one another. Head the board *Life of the Everglades*; use green construction paper as the background for the display. Begin the activity by showing the book index on an overhead projector. Ask student partners to choose to become experts about two or three of the items listed. They can do this by reading the pages referred to and by filling out these facts with further research in encyclopedias and non-fiction books. Partners can make cut-paper pictures of the plants and animals and place them appropriately on the bulletin board, with labels identifying them. As students contribute their work to the display, invite them to tell both what the plant or animal needs in order to live, and also how it is used by other life forms. Use the finished board as the basis for cause-and-effect investigations. For example, students can cover up an animal or plant and determine how the pattern of life in the Everglades would be disturbed if this life form disappeared. Invite students to review and then explain the impact that humans have on the Everglades ecosystem.

Making Connections

Research Skills:
On the Spot Arrange for the class to visit a local nature center to begin an investigation of animal habitats and the ecosystems in their area. As a goal of the trip, ask students to listen and look to find out how they can get involved in local environmental projects so that they become "stewards of the land." Back in the classroom, discuss ways students can educate others about what they have learned. This may include making posters and bumper stickers, drawing charts to show interrelationships, writing and distributing classroom *Weekly Earth Bulletin* to report on local problems and progress in regard to the environment, and writing letters to local editors to express their views.

Literature/Oral Language:
Finding Favorites Invite students to work individually or with a partner to find vivid descriptive passages in books about the earth and about animals and plants, and then read the material aloud to the class. Plan a *Words About Planet Earth* classroom period. Suggest that students practice their readings so that the class presentation can be recorded effectively on tape. Ask students to make copies of their selections to put in a folder on a reading table, and suggest that students read the selections as they listen to the tape.

Creative Writing:
What Do You See? Arrange an assortment of simple nature objects on a table and invite students to choose one to study and write about. Examples are: stones, leaves, flowers, seeds, seedpods, nuts, a cup of beach sand, shells, twigs, feathers. Suggest that students imagine that they are seeing the object for the very first time—as if they were a visitor from another planet—and examine the object thoroughly to become familiar with its shape, colors, texture, and size. Invite students to refer to the vocabulary notebook begun during the reading of *The Moon of the Alligator* to get ideas and inspirations for their own written descriptions. After students have read their work aloud to the class, display each piece of writing on a table by the object it describes. Suggest that students study the objects and read the descriptions with a partner.

Moon Calendar

For each month, draw a picture of a plant or animal you want to protect. Write the name of the plant or animal on the line. Show your calendar to a classmate and tell why each moon is important.

January	February	March
The Moon of the _____	The Moon of the _____	The Moon of the _____
April	**May**	**June**
The Moon of the _____	The Moon of the _____	The Moon of the _____
July	**August**	**September**
The Moon of the _____	The Moon of the _____	The Moon of the _____
October	**November**	**December**
The Moon of the _____	The Moon of the _____	The Moon of the _____

Name _____

The Alligator's World

1. On the lines, write words and phrases that describe alligators and their home.
2. Color the picture and cut it out.
3. With some classmates, bind your alligator cut-outs together to make the pages of a book. Read and show your book to your teacher or another group of classmates.

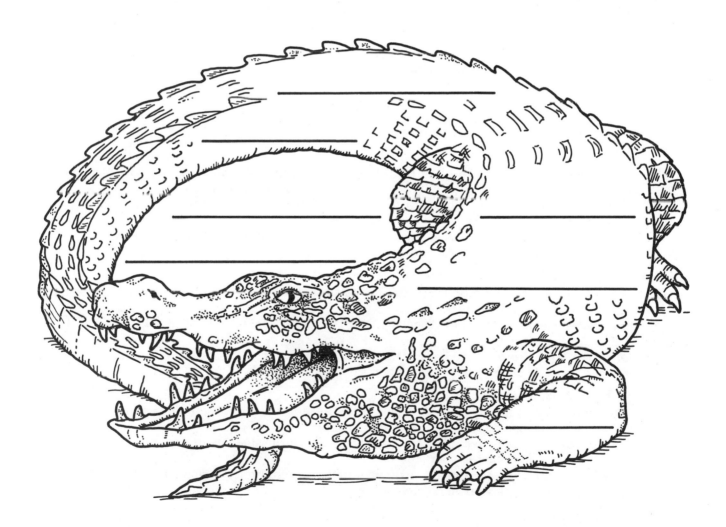

Additional Resources: Books for Your Students

The books listed here are among the many others that may also be used to reinforce geography skills and concepts. The list suggests books for all three reading-comprehension levels: Picture Books (Kindergarten–Grade 1); Story Books (Grade 1–Grade 2); Chapter Books (Grade 3–Grade 4). The notes suggest ways to use the book in your geography program.

1. Reading Picture Maps
- **(P)** *The Trip* Ezra Jack Keats (Greenwillow 1978). Students can make shoebox dioramas of their neighborhood.
- **(S)** *Winnie-the-Pooh* A. A. Milne (Dutton 1954). Use the end-paper maps to help students track story locales and to serve as a model for their own story maps.
- **(C)** *Stuart Little* E. B. White (Harper 1945). Invite students to draw a picture map showing the sites of Stuart's adventures.

2. Identifying Land Forms
- **(P)** *The Funny Little Woman* Arlene Mosel (Dutton 1972). Invite students to make cut-away diagrams showing what is on Earth's surface and what is below it.
- **(S)** *The Great Town and Country Bicycle Balloon Chase* Barbara Douglass (Lothrop 1984). Students can draw a bird's-eye view of what they would see on this journey.
- **(C)** *The Prince of the Dolomites* Tomie De Paola (Harcourt 1980). Invite students to enact a play about how a landform in your area came to be.

3. Noting Changes in Surroundings
- **(P)** *When I Was Young in the Mountains* Cynthia Rylant (Dutton 1982). Invite students to interview long-time residents to get information about changes in your community.
- **(S)** *Look Out, Patrick!* Paul Geraghty (Macmillan 1990). Students can re-tell the story using another animal-hero and setting other obstacles in his or her path.
- **(C)** *Ace: The Very Important Pig* Dick King-Smith (Crown 1990). Suggest that students study and sketch everyday surroundings from the point of view of another creature.

4. Identifying Native Animals
- **(P)** *Little Island* Margaret Wise Brown (O'Day 1946) Ask students to make a picture-list of animals and plants in their own surroundings.
- **(S)** *Dinosaur Garden* Liza Donnelly (Scholastic 1990) Invite students to find out what kids of animals lived in their region long ago.
- **(C)** *Hawk, I'm Your Brother* Byrd Baylor (Macmillan 1986) Suggest that cooperative learning groups write and illustrate a story about people interacting with wildlife.

5. Distinguishing Among Geographic Features
- **(P)** *Under Your Feet* Joanne Ryder (Four Winds 1990) Organize a nature walk during which students can find clues to living things that live underground.
- **(S)** *My Grandmother's Journey* John Cech (Bradbury 1991) Invite students to paint a mural that shows landforms and water in your area.
- **(C)** *In My Mother's House* Ann Nolan Clark (Puffin 1991) Cooperative learning groups can make picture maps showing people at work in different locations.

6. Identifying Resources
- **(P)** *Family Farm* Thomas Locker (Dial 1990) As a class project, students can raise money for a worthy cause by making simple things out of readily-available resources.

(S) *Corn Is Maize* Aliki (Harper 1976) Invite students to make a time-line tracing an ordinary product from its raw-material stage to their home or school.

(C) *On the Pampas* Maria Cristina Brusca (Holt 1991) Suggest that students make a picture chart comparing the resources in the book with ones in or near their own community.

7. Identifying Regions of the United States

(P) *Cows in the Parlor* Cynthia McFarland (Atheneum 1990) As a bulletin board project, students can help you complete a picture map showing where dairy cattle are raised.

(S) *Gila Monsters Meet You at the Airport* Marjorie Sharmat (Macmillan 1980) Invite cooperative learning groups to make true-false maps showing something outlandish and something factual about three or four regions of the country.

(C) *The Tree* Judy Hindley (Clarkson Potter 1990) Suggest that students identify regions of the United States through a picture-map showing trees native to the regions.

8. Noting Influence of Climate and Weather

(P) *The Winter Duckling* Keith Polette (Milliken 1990) Using the book as a pattern, students can tell stories about the duckling's adventures in other seasons.

(S) *Thunder Cake* Patricia Polacco (Philomel 1990) Invite cooperative learning groups to make classroom snacks and placemats celebrating various kinds of weather.

(C) *Mr. Popper's Penguins* Richard Atwater (Dell 1978) Invite students to write stories about how Mr. Popper would have to prepare for a visit to the Antarctic.

9. Noting Impact of Natural Forces

(P) *On the Day You Were Born* Debra Fraiser (Harcourt 1991) Invite students to make their own picture books about "what was going on in the universe" on the day they were born.

(S) *The Great Kapok Tree: A Tale of the Amazon Rain Forest* Lynne Cherry (Harcourt 1990) On a field trip around the community, students can look for ways in which humans are a "natural force" and later discuss ways in which this force changes the earth.

(C) *The Magic School Bus Inside the Earth* Joanna Cole (Scholastic 1987) Invite students to make cross-section drawings showing what is under the school.

10. Recognizing the Ocean as a Resource

(P) *The Whales' Song* Dyan Sheldon (Dial 1990) Play tape recordings of sounds made by marine mammals and invite students to paint pictures of what they hear.

(S) *Where the River Begins* Thomas Locker (Dial 1984) Suggest that students make maps tracing a major U.S. river to the sea.

(C) *Hattie and the Wild Waves* Barbara Cooney (Viking 1991) Invite cooperative learning groups to make montages of objects and cut-pictures that express the wonder and beauty of the ocean.

11. Recognizing People as Resources

(P) *My Perfect Neighborhood* Leah Komaiko (Harper 1990) Invite cooperative learning groups to make picture books showing both real and imaginary people in their own "perfect neighborhood."

(S) *Jafta's Mother, Jafta's Father, Jafta and the Wedding* Hugh Lewin (Carolrhoda Books 1981) Use the Jafta books as the basis for idea-webs showing how families and neighbors cooperate to get work done and to plan celebrations.

(C) *People of the Breaking Day* Marcia Sewall (Atheneum 1990) On a field trip to a local history museum, students can look for facts about Native American groups of their region that parallel the skills and activities of the Wampanoag.

12. Using Maps and Directional Words

(P) *The Red Balloon* A. Lamorisse (Doubleday 1956) Invite students to use the pictures to retell the story, using simple directional words (left, right, up, down, sideways, etc.) to tell where the balloon is going.

(S) *Cross-Country Cat* Mary Calhoun (Morrow 1979) Student partners can make maps of their community or state to show the cat's path if he were traveling cross-country in your area.

(C) *Miss Rumphius* Barbara Cooney (Viking 1982) Invite students to help you assemble a bulletin board that maps Miss Rumphius's journeys around the world.

13. Appreciating Natural Resources

(P) *Antarctica* Helen Cowcher (Farrar 1990) Cooperative learning groups can fill in an outline map of Antarctica with their own pictures of animals who live there.

(S) *The Lorax* Dr. Seuss (Random House 1971) Invite students to look and listen for news about forests today and write an *Our Forests* bulletin to distribute to other classrooms.

(C) *Urban Roosts: Where Birds Nest in the City* Barbara Bash (Sierra Club/Little Brown 1990) On a visit to a nature center, the class can find out about birds that frequent your area and how to build houses or feeders for some of them.

14. Identifying Changes

(P) *Shadows and Reflections* Tana Hoban (Greenwillow 1990) At two different times on a sunny day, invite students to make shadow pictures of objects on the playground. Discuss why the shadows are different as the day goes by.

(S) *Window* Jeannie Baker (Greenwillow 1991) Cooperative learning groups can work in teams to record changes seen through the classroom windows.

(C) *The Great Yellowstone Fire* Carole Vogel and Kathryn Goldner (Sierra Club/Little, Brown 1990) Invite students to make a Before-Right After-Finally picture chart that shows the changes and renewal that happened because of the fire.

15. Using a Globe

(P) *Under the Sun* Ellen Kandoian (Dodd 1987) Help students identify on a globe the places to which the story refers as the sun sets.

(S) *"Could Be Worse!"* James Stevenson (Greenwillow 1977) Invite students to show on a globe some possible locations of Grandpa's fantastic adventures.

(C) *Seeing the Earth from Space* Patricia Lauber (Orchard 1990) Student partners can locate on a globe the continents and oceans shown in these breathtaking photographs.

16. Recognizing Community Patterns

(P) *Not So Fast Songololo* Niki Daly (Puffin 1985) Invite students to use the book as a pattern for telling about an excursion of their own that they took with a relative.

(S) *The Potato Man* Megan McDonald (Watts 1991) On a field trip to a nearby shopping area, students can find parallels in modern communities and those of years past.

(C) *Hector Lives in the United States Now: The Story of a Mexican-American Child* Joan Hewett (Harper 1990) Suggest that students make a neighborhood map with pictures and labels on it for new classmates who come from other lands and would appreciate an introduction to their new home.

17. Understanding Natural Cycles

(P) *Great Northern Diver: The Loon* Barbara Juster Esbensen (Little 1991) Invite students to use graphic organizers to show how other animals, or humans, adapt to the changing seasons.

(S) *Song of the Swallows* Leo Politi (Macmillan 1948) Invite students to help you organize a picture map display or time line showing where the swallows are at different times of the year.

(C) *Many Moons* James Thurber (Harcourt 1971) Cooperative learning groups can extend the story by giving a play about the princess, the moon, and the cycle of tides.

18. Tracing Exploration Routes

(P) *The Journey Home* Alison Lester (Houghton 1991) Suggest that students make picture maps tracing the fantastic voyage of Wild and Woolly.

(S) *A Picture Book of Christopher Columbus* David Adler (Holiday 1991) Ask students to help you assemble a picture map on the bulletin board tracing Columbus's voyages.

(C) *The Discovery of the Americas* Betsy Maestro (Lothrop 1991) Suggest that student partners make time-lines that show the sequence of exploration, which begins in this book with Stone Age peoples crossing the Bering Land Bridge.

19. Studying Competing Uses of Land

(P) *Evan's Corner* Elizabeth Starr Hill (Viking 1991) Invite students to draw illustrated floorplans showing how Evan and his family learn to share a small space.

(S)*Shaker Lane* Alice and Martin Provensen (Viking 1987) On a neighborhood field trip, students can make notes about and draw pictures of old and new buildings in their community.

(C)*The Boy Who Held Back the Sea* Thomas Locker (Dial 1987) Invite cooperative learning groups to make word and picture reports about other instances in which humans and other natural forces (in this story, the ocean) seem to compete for use of the land.

20. Comparing Topographical and Political Maps

(P)*Angel Child, Dragon Child* Michelle Sarat (Scholastic 1989) Invite students to find Vietnam and the United States on a map and a globe.

(S)*How Many Days To America?* Eve Bunting (Clarion 1988) Student can first locate the starting point and destination on a political map, then use a topographical map to get an idea of the hazards the refugees faced during their boat journey.

(C)*Mufaro's Beautiful Daughters* John Steptoe (Lothrop 1987) Invite students to find Zimbabwe on both a political and topographical map, then discuss how the illustrations give a close-up view of the topography.

21. Studying Regional Likenesses and Differences

(P)*Country Crossing* Jim Aylesworth (Atheneum 1991) Invite students to extend the story by telling what the passengers on a train might see as they leave the country and ride to the city.

(S)*At the Crossroads* Rachel Isadora (Greenwillow 1991) Discuss how the South African landscape is different from the one in your area, and how homecoming celebrations are the same.

(C)*Sierra* Diane Siebert (HarperCollins 1991) Cooperative learning groups can do research to find out how the topography of their region, too, has changed from the ice ages to the present.

22. Exploring a Continent

(P)*Before You Came This Way* Byrd Baylor (Dutton 1990) Students can make a picture map showing ancient Native American life in the Southwest.

(S)*Jambo Means Hello: A Swahili Alphabet Book* Muriel Feelings (Dial 1974) Provide students with copies of the map in the book and invite them to label and decorate it with scenes and words from African village life.

(C)*Oh, the Places You'll Go!* Dr. Seuss (Random House 1990) On a bulletin board map of the world, students can put labels and pictures of places they want to visit on all the continents.

23. Exploring Mountain Ranges

(P)*The Mountain* Peter Parnall (Doubleday 1971). Invite a park or forest ranger to visit the classroom and tell about the animals and plants that live on the mountain or in the hilly region nearest your area.

(S)*Wheel on the Chimney* Margaret Wise Brown (Lippincott 1955) Invite students to trace on a map or globe the route the storks follow and the mountains they fly above as they migrate between Africa and Hungary.

(C)*The Moon of the Gray Wolves* Jean Craighead George (HarperCollins 1991) Invite interested students to use maps to find the Alaskan Range and the Toklat Pass, then draw and label a picture diagram to illustrate main sites in the story.

24. Appreciating Ecosystems

(P)*Bear* John Schoenherr (Philomel 1991) Invite students to make additional illustrations for the story showing the animals and plants in the young bear's environment.

(S)*Woodpile* Peter Parnall (Macmillan 1990) On a field trip to a wooded park or on a guided nature walk, students can look for signs of abundant life in small areas.

(C)*Brother Eagle, Sister Sky* Illustrated by Susan Jeffers (Dial 1991) Invite students to choose some of Chief Seattle's words and paint their own pictures to accompany the words.

Teacher Resources

Professional Books and Articles

1. Cudd, E. T. and Roberts, L. Using Writing To Enhance Content Learning in the Primary Grades. *The Reading Teacher,* 42 (1989), 392–405.

2. Goodland, J. *A Place Called School.* New York: McGraw-Hill 1984.

3. Ogle, D. M. The Know, Want To Know, Learn Strategy. In K. D. Muth (Ed.), *Children's Comprehension of Text.* Newark, Delaware: International Reading Association 1989.

4. Readence, J. E., Bean, T. W., and Baldwin, R. S. *Content Area Reading: An Integrated Approach* (3rd ed.) Dubuque, Iowa: Kendall/Hunt 1989.

5. Vacca, R. T. and Vacca, J. L. *Content Area Reading* (2nd ed.) Boston, Massachusetts: Little, Brown 1986.

Periodicals Often Featuring Bibliographies of Curriculum Links

Booklinks   *The Five Owls*   *The Horn Book*   *Perspectives*

Geography Reference Books You Can Use With Your Students

Single-Volume Encyclopedias:

1. *The Random House Children's Encyclopedia* (Random House 1991) Vivid maps, photographs, and "fact finder" charts.

2. *Exploring Your World: The Adventure of Geography* (National Geographic Society 1989) Physical and human geography, spectacular maps and illustrations.

3. *The Doubleday Children's Almanac* (Doubleday 1986) Twelve subject-sections, many of them linked to geography.

Atlases:

1. *My First Atlas* by Kate Petty (Warner 1991) Bright, detailed maps and illustrations, plus "fact capsules" and quizzes that are fun.

2. *Reader's Digest Children's World Atlas* (Random House 1991) Maps and illustrations of the world's peoples, wildlife, and terrain.

3. *Concise Earth Book World Atlas* (Earthbooks 1990) A little book (5″ × 7″) packed with beautiful maps and charts.